# THE BANK ROBBER'S BOY

## PETER NORRIS

Big Sky Publishing Pty Ltd
PO Box 303, Newport, NSW 2106, Australia
Phone: 1300 364 611
Email: info@bigskypublishing.com.au
Web: www.bigskypublishing.com.au

Cover design: Think Productions

 A catalogue record for this
book is available from the
National Library of Australia

Title: The Bank Robber's Boy
ISBN: 978-1-923144-85-9

# THE BANK ROBBER'S BOY

BIG SKY PUBLISHING
www.bigskypublishing.com.au

**PETER NORRIS**

## Content Warning

This book contains accounts of traumatic events, including themes of violence, abuse, and emotional hardship, which may be distressing to some readers. Please prioritise your wellbeing and take breaks as needed. If you need support, consider reaching out to your local mental health services.

# CONTENTS

# PETER NORRIS' OPEN LETTER TO THE STATE GOVERNMENT OF VICTORIA.

In April 2024 Peter Norris was not permitted to read this statement at his hearing. The State representatives cited WHS reasons for this decision "it was too difficult for them to hear".

My name is Peter Norris.

At the outset, I acknowledge that not one person in this room is responsible for the horrific crimes committed against me during my time at Baltara Reception Centre.

The uncomfortable truths I share with you today – however difficult to hear – slice deeper than any of the physical wounds I have suffered. My lived experiences at Baltara have morphed into painful memories; ghosts that will haunt me until the day I die.

As a child of the state, this government stood as my legal guardian. You were supposed to be my surrogate parents and protectors. Instead, you fed me to the wolves.

I was just a small boy when the officer at Shepparton Police Station told me through sobbing breaths that I was being sent to a juvenile detention centre because there was nowhere else for me to go. My father had just been incarcerated and, through no fault of my own, I was set to suffer the same fate. I hugged the police officer as she cried, put on my best game face, and said: "Don't worry Miss, I'll be OK".

How I wish those words didn't mock me still.

Unbeknown to that vulnerable little boy, I would not be OK.

Far from it.

My innocence would be ripped from under my tiny wings; my childhood stolen.

I understand that my placement at Baltara is not something I can be compensated for. But as a victim and a survivor, the horrific acts of abuse I endured there must be voiced and remedied. Not just for me, but for all the other kids whose lives were shattered before they even had a chance to begin.

I ask you this:

If it was your child, wrenched from their bed in the dead of night, stripped naked and beaten until they soiled themselves just for the crime of crying – what compensation would you demand for such brutality?

If it was your little one's head being shoved underwater, their desperate gasps for breath and cries for help met with mirth from the very people entrusted to care for them – what price could you begin to put on that torture?

And if it was your baby being digitally raped; their battered body left to bleed on a cold, hard floor, what restitution could ever untarnish their stolen virtue?

For 35 years, the abuse I suffered as a child of this state stunted my spirit; my self-worth was decimated. A boy with boundless dreams and potential reduced to a hollow husk, convinced my only lot in life was to be the world's punching bag. It has taken lifetimes to claw my way out of the abyss, to reclaim any fragment of the man I was meant to become.

I don't blame you for the sins of your predecessors – but I do pray you have evolved beyond them. I implore you to look me in the eyes today and bear witness to the human cost of your failures.

The state promised to nurture me and keep me safe.

Yet it shattered my spirit and tarnished my soul.

I ask only that you find within yourselves the moral fortitude to deliver justice that can start healing what no child should ever endure.

My name is Peter Norris. When you go home tonight, as you tuck your babies into bed, I hope you'll remember my name and my story. A story that shapes a history that should never be repeated.

Thank you for listening.

*The life you seek is discovered in the brave choices you are willing to make.*

# PREFACE

Some dads coach junior footy. Others clock in 9-5. My dad?

My dad was a bank robber who outfoxed the law for two decades.

From Sydney's sun-drenched harbour to Melbourne's shadowy streets, he pocketed millions between 1965 and 1985, leaving chaos in his wake. Dad wasn't just notorious for his robberies – he was legendary for his escapes. One of the first to bust out of Sydney's Long Bay Jail, he turned dodging the police into a twisted kind of talent.

For years, my siblings and I were unwitting accomplices, dragged along on a cross-country crime spree. We told ourselves we didn't *really* know what the old man was up to – whether that was true or just a comforting lie, I still can't say.

Even now, with the full weight of his crimes heavy on my shoulders, I can't shake my love for him. This messy, complicated love drives me to chase a life of better choices; to prove that a father's legacy doesn't have to be a life sentence for his kids.

I didn't write this story to glorify Dad or his crimes. I wrote it to prove to myself, and to the world, that I am more than the sum of my father's misdeeds. This is me saying: I'm more than what I was back then. I'm more than the Bank Robber's Boy.

# CHAPTER 1

# A SILENT CAR RIDE

My brother Dave remembers Dad being handcuffed and hauled away by the police early one morning. He must have been seven at the time. Of the four kids, he was the oldest. Tina came next – she was five – then Kelly, three, then me. I was an infant at the time.

Dave remembers that we had spent the last few months hiding out at Mum's parents' place in Kellyville. He doesn't remember much about the property, only that it had old cars in the yard, chickens, a couple of goats and a dog. The dog's name was Codie. He was a mutt. Dave, Tina and Kelly played with him for hours at a time, while I sat watching from my Baby Bouncer.

Pop had built the house himself. It was large but basic, and always smelled like pine, a smell that grew stronger on hot days. We were bathed in a tin tub on the porch until Pop gave in and built a small bath. It was concrete and Dave remembers it felt rough on his arse. Pop's hands were rough, too, when he bathed him, but he never questioned that the old man loved him. Even at five, Dave knew our grandparents loved us more than our mother.

The day the cops took Dad away, Mum shouted and swore at them, then locked herself in her childhood bedroom. Dave played with the girls and Codie, then came inside to eat at the formica dining table with Nan and Pop. When Kelly said she wanted to give Mum a cuddle, Nan said she needed her rest.

Dave has no idea how long Dad was gone that time. When he finally came back, though, he didn't mention the cops or the arrest. He said he'd been down in Tasmania cutting trees for a big logging company. He showed Dave a long, puffy scar on his upper back and said it was from an axe wound. A couple of weeks later, Dave remembers hearing him tell the girls he got the scar fighting off a bear. They were too young to know that Australia didn't have bears.

As young kids, we moved around a lot. Shortly after Dad came home, we found ourselves in a blonde brick semi-detached house in the Sydney suburb of Summer Hill. As was usually the case, our houses were housing commission, simple without any of the modern amenities or appliances many other families had, but Dave doesn't remember complaining. So long as we were all together, he was happy.

At the blonde brick house, Mum and Dad had lots of parties – barbeques, where people would arrive in the early afternoon and wouldn't leave until the following day. One of Dad's best friends at this time was named George, but Dad and his other friends called him 'The Kid'.

Dave remembers visiting George's house too. It was much bigger than ours, in a much nicer neighbourhood. He even had a games room, complete with billiard table. On one visit, Dave picked up the cue to play, but Dad said he was too young and would rip the felt. Then George came over. He showed Dave how to use and hold the cue, with a forefinger over the stick for safety. Dave completely fluked it and sunk three reds on his first shot. All the men cheered and laughed. Dave remembers how proud Dad looked. He was always allowed to play billiards after that.

Thinking back now, it seems obvious that most of Dad's friends were criminals. 'George' was George Freeman, whom Dad met while they were locked up in Grafton Jail. Grafton was notorious for its brutality, both from inmates and from prison officers wielding rubber batons. George had gone to jail when he was only eighteen, and apparently Dad and his mates had taken the young and vulnerable George under their wings and got him working alongside them in the bakehouse. After they got out of jail, George rose quickly through the criminal ranks, while Dad – for all his faults – remained in the background. I like to imagine that this decision was about protecting his family, although that may be wishful thinking.

Whenever we moved, we changed names. Dave remembers having to introduce himself as Dave Gregg, Dave Wright, Dave Reynolds. He prided himself on never making a mistake, although the girls weren't so lucky.

Dave thinks the family went by Reynolds when we moved to the Melbourne suburb of Sunshine. He had only just been enrolled at Sunshine Primary School and had made his first friend when the police came for Dad again. Last time, he had only seen them from a distance. This time, there was a policeman in his bedroom when he woke up early in the morning. He wore a suit, but as he stretched to search the top of Dave's wardrobe, Dave saw the handcuffs clipped to his belt.

Dave jumped out of bed and ran towards the lounge room. As he passed the girls' room, he smelled the acrid stench of old nappies and saw both girls sitting on their beds, being supervised by a uniformed female officer.

Dave found mum in the lounge room. She was sitting on the couch, crying. When he put his hand on her shoulder, she recoiled.

'Where's Dad?' he asked, but she didn't answer and he already knew. Dad was gone.

This time, he hadn't been arrested. He'd done a runner.

A couple of nights later, Dave was woken by the sound of a man's voice in the hallway. As he opened his eyes, his bedroom door opened. He squinted against the glare. Dad stood there, his dark brown hair and stocky shoulders silhouetted against the light. 'Davey?'

'Mmmm,' Davey muttered sleepily.

'You've got five minutes to get dressed. Pack what you can. Leave the rest.'

Obediently, Dave slipped on his jeans, t-shirt and tennis shoes, then started packing. He took his record player, three prized 45s, and some clothes, all of which he shoved into his school bag, while Mum raced up and down the hall, tossing things in a rucksack for the rest of us. Dad came back for Dave and took him by the hand, then led him to the white Monaro in the driveway. It was still covered with fingerprint powder.

For a couple of weeks after that, Dave remembers the family hiding out at a racehorse stud and agistment farm with one of Dad's mates, a guy named Kenny Stocken. Once they'd put the city behind them, the tension between Mum and Dad had seemingly evaporated. Life on the farm was great, particularly for Dave. Being the oldest, he was allowed to drive a converted lawnmower, which towed a trailer filled with horse feed. Then, just as suddenly as we'd arrived, we left again. Dave never found out why, but he didn't question it. It was just the way things were.

Mum and Dad took us to Garners Avenue, Marrickville, where Dave and Tina were enrolled at the local school under the surname 'Norris'. This was my mum's maiden name. It's the name I use today.

Dave doesn't remember much about the school, but he remembers being picked up by Dad and a mate one afternoon. They were driving a small truck, so the three of them were crammed into the cabin. They drove out of town, until housing estates turned to paddocks. At some point, Dad motioned to something up ahead, and his friend said, 'Yep. I see it.' They pulled up alongside a big red truck loaded with bales of hay. Opening his door, Dad climbed down from the cabin and sauntered towards the red truck.

'Where's he going?' Dave asked, more curious than worried.

'Don't you worry,' Dad's friend said. 'He's good at this. One of the best.'

Dave had no idea what the man was talking about. He watched Dad walk the length of the red truck, then glance into the cabin. Having done so, he turned around and scanned the road, then the neighbouring fields. Finally, he turned towards his mate and Dave and shrugged, then grinned. Moments later, he was opening the passenger side door, then pulling himself up and into the red truck's cabin. Dave waited, holding his breath. The red truck's engine spluttered once … twice … then roared to life.

For the next few minutes, both trucks drove along the highway at a sensible pace. Then Dad indicated left, and Dave watched him make a tight turn onto a dirt road. As they followed the red truck's lead, Dave saw dust rise behind the truck's wheels and tiny fragments of dirt fell on the windscreen between them.

In this secluded spot, both trucks stopped, and Dave watched the men unload the hay off the back of the red truck and onto Dad's mate's truck. Then his mate climbed back into the cabin. His red face ran with sweat. Dave didn't like the way he smelled, and moved slightly further away from him while he watched Dad.

What Dad was doing now confused him. In one hand he had a newspaper, in the other his cigarette lighter. For a moment, Dave wondered whether he was going to sit down and have a smoke while reading the paper like he sometimes did, but that didn't make sense.

While Dave watched in awe, Dad rolled up the newspaper, lit one end, and walked to the open passenger window of the big red truck, where he tossed it inside. Then he sauntered back to his mate's truck and climbed in beside Dave. 'Alright,' he told his mate, then ruffled Dave's hair. Unlike his mate, Dad didn't look hot and sweaty. He was still grinning.

They drove back down the dirt path, and were turning onto the highway when Dave heard a dull roar from somewhere behind him. He jumped, and looked up at Dad, who winked. As they drove down the highway, he followed Dad's gaze and watched a plume of thick black smoke curl up from the clearing deep inside the bush.

Dave didn't tell Mum or the girls about the truck. It was his secret. Whenever he thought about it, it gave him a little thrill, but it also made him worried. He kept expecting the police to show up again. Maybe, this time, they would ask *him* what he'd seen. What would he say then?

Despite his fears, life in Marrickville was remarkably uneventful. Over the weeks that followed, Dad got a job as a cleaner at the Petersham Private Hospital and even took Dave to work with him a couple of times. It was on one of these occasions that Dave saw Dad watching the security guards. He had stopped cleaning and there was an intensity to his expression that made Dave worried all over again.

Dave doesn't remember exactly when, or how, he found out what happened at Petersham. According to news reports, however, one morning two armed men wearing balaclavas robbed the hospital's payroll, which was said to be around $10,000, a substantial amount in those days. Perhaps it was no surprise that we were soon on the move again, this time to Blacktown. Dave and Tina attended Seven Hills West Primary. Dave was enrolled in Grade 2, while Kelly had just started Prep. She cried a lot whenever he had to leave her. At recess and lunch, he would rather play cricket or footy, but he sat with her. He knew Dad would have flogged him if he heard otherwise.

After a few months in Blacktown, we were permitted to rent a housing commission unit. I had recently celebrated my first birthday and had begun to walk. For hours at a time, I pushed my toy wheel barrow around the yard, while Kelly played and occasionally caught snails, which she then ate, their squirming bodies bubbling over her lips as she spat out their broken shells. Dad had used some of his proceedings from the burglary to buy Dave an air rifle, which they used to shoot at cans in the backyard.

Compared to our last few houses, this one was nice. It was solid brick and filled with new furniture. It even had a pool table in the lounge room. This wasn't as fancy as George's billiard table, but Dave still loved it.

My parents hosted parties regularly, including card nights, attended mostly by Dad's mates. One of these mates was Darcy Dugan. As I would learn years later, he was famous for committing many armed holdups, but gained more notoriety as a prison escape artist. His biggest escape, however, was when he had his death sentence commuted to life imprisonment. When he was partying at our place, he must have been on the run, but if he was worried about being recaptured, he didn't show it. Dave remembers him as the ultimate larrikin, full of fun and laughter.

Even though life was good, Dave still felt on edge. It was a sunny day when Dad packed the kids into the car – at the time, a bright yellow VW - and told them they were going for a drive. They had been driving for what felt like a long time when Dad told Dave that he and mum weren't getting along.

When he heard this, Dave realised what his anxiety had been about. 'Are you going to split up?' he asked.

Dad paused for a moment, then said, 'We already did, mate. She's been seeing some bloke she met at the pub.' He didn't sound angry, just disappointed.

Dave doesn't remember hearing about lawyers or anybody fighting for custody. It seemed like Mum and Dad just made an arrangement. We would live with Dad most of the time, but would still get to see mum once a fortnight. Each Friday, Dad would drive two kids over to mum's boyfriend's place in Mount Druitt, where they would stay until Sunday evening.

Mum's boyfriend's name was Tim. He was an ex-commando from England, with short-cropped hair and thick muscles across his chest and shoulders. When Tim saw that Dave was interested in soldiers and guns, he tried to strike up a friendship, but Dave formed an instant dislike for Tim out of loyalty to Dad.

One weekend, instead of having Dad drop the kids at the house in Mount Druitt, Mum and Tim drove over to our house to pick up Dave and Tina. The four of them drove to Manly, where Tim had splashed out on a couple of hotel rooms. On Saturday, he gave Dave a two dollar note and told him he could spend it however he liked. Dave visited the shops that lined the esplanade and the fun park on the pier, and bought an ice cream, which he ate while sitting on the warm sand on his own.

The next morning, at around 6:30am, Dave woke up and walked through the door that separated his and Tina's room from Mum's. In the half-light, he didn't know what he was seeing at first: the shapes moving under the sheets. Then Tim noticed him by the door and climbed off mum. Reaching into the bedside table, he pulled out his wallet and removed another two-dollar note. When Dave remained where he was, Tim said, 'Come on, what're you waiting for?' Dave crossed the room and took the two-dollar note from the man's hand. Before he left, he heard Tim say, 'Now get lost!'

As he had done the previous day, Dave walked down to the pier, but the park wasn't open yet. Then he had another idea. With the two-dollar note, he bought a ticket for the ferry and caught it from Manly to Circular Quay. Then he found a taxi rank and climbed into the first cab he found. When he gave the driver our address in Blacktown, the driver asked how much money Dave had. Dave showed him the change he'd received for his two dollars from the ferry conductor, and the driver told him it would cost a lot more than that.

Walking to a nearby phone box, Dave called Dad. He explained what had happened, and Dad told him to bring the taxi driver to the phone. Minutes later, Dave was sitting in the cab as it crawled through the city on its way to Blacktown. As Dave disembarked, Dad walked out of the house and paid the driver, then tapped the tin roof of the taxi and watched it drive off.

Inside, over hot milo, Dad asked Dave a lot of questions. Then he roughly tousled his hair and told him he'd done the right thing coming home. 'Keep an eye on Kelly and Peter when they wake up, would you?' he said. Then he switched on the TV and left the house. Moments later, Dave heard a car door slam shut and Dad's VW peeled out of the driveway.

Later that afternoon, Dad came back with Tina, whom he led by the hand. Dave wasn't surprised to see them, but he *was* surprised to see Mum. She walked behind Dad and Tina, her face ashen, her head down.

A couple of days later, when everything had settled down and Dave had the chance to ask him what happened, Dad said that Tim wasn't so tough after all. When Dad showed up, he'd refused to open the hotel door, so Dad used a tomahawk to smash it in. Then he turned the weapon around and used it on Tim's skull.

Dave must have looked shocked, because Dad said, 'He'll be alright. Just knocked a bit of sense into him.' Using his knuckles, he made a hollow knocking sound on the side of his own head.

Although the family was together again, Dave noticed how much Mum cried over the next few days. She hardly spoke, and whenever he happened to walk into a room where she was on her own, she seemed to be staring into space. One night, Dave woke up to hear commotion in the house, and saw Dad and a neighbour carrying her, fully clothed, into the shower, where they ran cold water over her limp body. Finally, she woke up, screaming as she tried to make sense of what was happening.

They eased her out of the tub, but she was shaking violently, and as Dad closed the bathroom door Dave watched her slump to the floor once more.

It was while mum was still recovering from what Dad called her 'breakdown' that another one of his mates came to live with us. Dad told us to call him Uncle Billy. His wife's name was Evette. Uncle Billy was skinny, with coke bottle glasses, and looked like the quintessential nerd. Even at age seven, Dave wondered how a guy like Billy had managed to find a wife like Evette. She had gently curled blond hair, wore bright red lipstick, and had big breasts that she showed off in brightly-coloured halter tops.

Uncle Billy was Billy Harrison, and along with Neddy Smith, was known as one of the best street fighters getting around Sydney in the 80's.

One night, Uncle Billy and Evette had offered to shout the family to fish and chips. Dad had just placed our order when three bikies entered the shop, proudly showing their colours. They immediately turned their attention to Evette. One of them asked whether she'd like a ride on his Harley. At first, Billy ignored them. The man asked again. Dave watched Evette's cheeks redden. Billy politely asked the men to stop being rude and to just let them eat in peace, but they laughed it off, one of them placing his thick fingers on Billy's shoulders and giving him a squeeze that made the smaller man wince.

'Alright,' Dad said, after watching the scene. 'I think we'll head home.'

Dave was disappointed. He'd hardly eaten any of his dinner. But there was something in Dad's voice that told him not to argue. Dave, Tina and Kelly left the shop ahead of Mum and Dad. Dad was carrying me. Evette had left too, and was walking with mum.

They were half a block from the fish and chip shop when Dave heard a crash and looked back to see one of the bikies fly through the plate-glass window. There was the sound of something breaking inside the shop, as well, before Billy emerged, dragging another of the men. As the bikie begged him to stop, Billy pushed his bearded cheek onto the shattered glass that littered the pavement. Then he began raking the man's face back and forth. The last thing Billy did was to collect the food he had ordered for everybody. According to Dave, we ate the fish and chips at home. They were a bit cold, and the newspaper in which they were wrapped were covered in blood, but nobody seemed to mind.

Uncle Billy and Evette slept in mine and Dave's room, so we slept in the living room, Dave on the couch, me in my cot. Dave remembers that he was often woken by Dad's voice, angry and guttural, and Mum's plaintive cries in response. One night, he heard Dad demanding, 'What did you tell him? What did you fucking tell him?' Then he heard the unmistakable sound of Dad's bolt-action .22 being cocked and Dad asked the same question again, much softer this time. Dave couldn't hear mum's answer, only her whimpering.

Instinctively, Dave knew who Dad meant by 'him'. Tim. Mum's ex-boyfriend. He understood immediately that Tim was threatening to stir up trouble for the family. This was confirmed a couple of days later, when Dave heard Dad and Uncle Billy talking. Billy asked whether Dad wanted him to 'get rid of the cunt.' Dad seemed to think about it for a while, then said no.

Rather than admiring Dad for showing restraint, Dave felt angry. He had never liked Tim. Why should he have the right to hurt the family, maybe separate them? For the first time, Dave felt ashamed of Dad in that moment, of his weakness for not allowing Billy to do what had to be done.

The following week, Uncle Billy and Evette left for Townsville. The next morning, Dave woke up to hear the chirping of birds, but he immediately knew something wasn't right. He climbed out of bed and walked down the hallway. He could hear Tina and Kelly crying. As he entered the lounge room, detectives were walking Dad down the front stairs, his hands cuffed behind him. This time, Dave didn't cry. Neither did Mum.

A couple of hours later, Pop turned up in his Chrysler. He told all of us to grab what we needed, so Dave collected his air rifle, some clothes and his bike, and packed them in the back of the car, along with everybody else's belongings. Pop drove us to his place. He and Nan had recently sold the Kellyville property and moved out to smaller plot at Dural. Nobody talked much.

The following day was April 12th 1975. Mum said she was going shopping, hugged us all and left.

It was the last time we saw her.

## Chapter 2

# THE DAY WE WERE TORN APART

We had been living at Nan and Pop's place for three months with no word from mum.

Pop worked at the local timber yard. One Friday afternoon, he came home, parked his car in front of the garage as usual, then sat in his car for a few minutes. Finally, he opened his door, then made his way slowly along the veranda, his feet sounding heavy and hollow. At least that's how Dave remembers it.

Pop entered the house without a word.

While Dave and Tina played cards in the living room, Pop put on the kettle. It was when he scolded himself that Dave knew something was wrong.

For a long time, Pop stood at the faucet, washing his red-streaked hand, staring out the window at the bush beyond. Dave watched his back – the slump of his shoulders – and tried to think of something to say. Then Pop went to the hall that led to our bedrooms.

Nan was on the porch, where Kelly played in the dirt just beyond her reach. Every couple of minutes, Kelly would toss dirt in the air, and Nan would tell her to stop it. Otherwise, she was silent.

Finally, Pop carried three big bags through the living room and dropped them on the porch. Dave looked over, and saw the look Pop exchanged with Nan: the tight lips, the creased forehead. Then he said, 'Kids, onto the porch.'

We sat on the faded wooden porch boards while Pop spoke to us in a soft, serious voice. He explained that mum wouldn't be coming back. Dave said he had been expecting to hear this for months, so it wasn't exactly a surprise, but he still found himself crying. Dave was sitting on Nan's knee, something he wasn't usually allowed to do because he was too big. She was crying too. He could feel her body shaking against his back.

Only I didn't cry. I was still too young to understand.

'Right,' Pop said, after a couple of minutes, as the girls' sobs threatened to become wails. He slapped his big hands on the faced knees of his jeans and pushed himself into a standing position. 'That's enough sooking.' He looked at Nan when he said that. She started to cry harder and made her way round the side of the house. 'In the car, you lot.'

Dave carried me to the car and put me in the back seat between my sisters. Tina buckled me in. Then Pop started the engine and opened his window, clearly looking for Nan. He honked the horn twice. When she didn't reappear, he pressed the accelerator and the car tore out of the driveway.

Halfway down the highway on the road into town, Kelly started to cry again. Dave turned around in his seat and held her hand, and she calmed down. I stared out the window, naming the things I saw: 'Tree.' 'Bird.' 'Grass.'

After only a few minutes, Pop pulled into the expansive parking lot of the local Seventh-Day Adventist Church. He had begun attending in the late forties and was now a senior member. Whenever we had visited the church before, it had been during service, when arriving late meant standing in the back. On a Friday evening, the church was almost empty. Only a couple of parishioners were in attendance. Pop greeted them by name, exchanged some pleasantries, then begged off and took us to the parish house, an office above the knave.

To this day, I am still not certain of the legalities around what happened next. After a brief meeting with the priest, we were led back to the rectory, where three families stood in self-contained huddles, waiting for something. Then the priest nodded to the father of one of the families and he approached the pew where I sat.

It was as the man reached for me that Tina realised what was about to happen. She leapt forward and grabbed me, hugging me to her chest and backing away from the man. Then she grabbed Kelly with her free hand and wrapped an arm tightly around her, but it was no use. As the man pried me from Tina's fingers, the priest held her shoulders. Dave stood by helplessly, pale and shaking.

Within minutes, the four of us had been separated. Kelly, Tina and I had been taken – 'adopted' – by parish families, while Dave remained with Nan and Pop.

Pop had hated my dad for a long time for the way he had treated Mum. By placing us with separate families, and without a paper trail or formal adoption process, he must have figured it would be almost impossible for my dad to find us when he was released from jail. I guess he thought he was protecting us, but his actions would have repercussions that continue to this day.

*

As harrowing as I'm sure that day in the church was for me at the time, I have no memory of it. Instead, I remember nothing of my life with the Robinsons until I was around four. Looking back now, I can see them, and still feel the sense of attachment I had for them. I assumed they were *my* family. There was Bill (Dad), Jane (Mum) and my siblings John, Matthew and Karen.

We lived in a modest and immaculately clean house in the suburbs of Sydney. I had clothes, toys, and plenty of food to eat. I even had my own bedroom.

We attended church regularly, often more than once a week. When they met a new parishioner for the first time, Bill or Jane would always introduce us the same way: 'These are our children,' one of them would say. 'John, Matthew and Karen. And this is Peter, our Gift from God.'

One day, after church, I was thinking about this expression – wondering why God had chosen me to be his gift – when I felt a warm rush from my nose, and looked down to see blood trickling down the front of my favourite Spiderman t-shirt and onto mum's teal velvet couch. 'Mum!' I called, worried. She walked in, then knelt quickly and told me to put my head back. Immediately, blood flooded the back of my throat, and I spluttered, but she held the bridge of my nose and in a couple of minutes her touch seemed to stem the flow.

This was the first blood nose of many. One night, I awoke to find my pillow wet under my cheek. I wondered whether I had dribbled in my sleep. Then I turned my bedside lamp on and noticed that pillow case and pyjama top were soaked with blood. Holding the bridge of my nose like mum had showed me, I tiptoed down the hallway and entered my parents' room.

Mum always slept on the left side of the bed. I tapped her on the shoulder. She stirred and mumbled something, then opened her eyes. When she saw me covered in blood, she let out a yelp, then covered her mouth and marched me out of the room. In my bedroom, she stared at the bloody pillowcase, shaking her head.

'Oh Peter,' she whispered, 'What have you done?'

I was confused. I knew I had been getting a lot of blood noses recently, but I couldn't help it. I was about to try to explain this when I heard heavy footfalls in the hallway and Dad stormed in the room. 'What's going on, Peter?' he yelled. 'Why are you always *doing* this?'

His reaction startled me. I started to cry, my cheeks suddenly wet with tears, blood and snot hanging in long strings from my nose and chin. 'I'm sorry,' I said, helplessly. 'I'm sorry.'

As my mum left the room in search of fresh linen, I was left with my dad. He stared down at me for a few moments in silence, his face reddening as I continued to cry. Then he turned on his heel and left the room. As I heard his footsteps recede down the carpeted passageway, my tears began to subside, and my heart stopped racing. I was surprised when the door opened wide and, instead of Mum, I saw it was Dad. He was holding his black, shiny belt – the one he wore to the office.

His mouth was set in a straight line. He took a deep breath, then said, 'Face the wall.' In silence, I did as he told me. I could hear his breathing as he approached: heavy and ragged. Then he said, 'Pants.'

Dad had never hit me before, but instinctively I knew what he meant. I lowered my pants, exposing my underpants and, below them, my bare legs.

CRACK!

The sound reverberated and I felt the cold flash of pain as leather met the backs of my thighs.

I screamed in shock.

'Shush!' he shouted, his voice as sharp as the strap.

I fell silent again, hoping that my obedience would stop the punishment.

CRACK!

The second blow hurt more than the first. This time, I felt my body sag, and had to brace myself against the wall to remain standing. Then his hand was on my collar, pulling me upright, repositioning me for the next strike.

I don't know how many times he hit me that night. I don't know when I stopped crying. I remember the backs of my legs burning, and the way he grunted each time he hit me. Then my vision started to black around the edges and I sagged again and he let me fall. As I turned around, I saw his sweaty face above me.

As soon as Dad left the room, Mum came back. She made my bed, efficient as always, removing the soiled linen and replacing it with a fitted sheet and top sheet that smelled like talc. She tucked the corners in tightly before smoothing out the bedspread and folding it over once. Finally, she motioned for me to remove my top. When I was unable to do so without assistance, she stepped forward and removed the blood-soaked garment in a deft move, then wiped my nose with a clean handkerchief she kept in her dressing gown pocket.

We sat beside each other as she lowered a fresh pyjama top over my head. Then she pulled the coverlet up just enough for me to enter. I climbed in, and winced as the backs of my legs touched the sheet beneath me. She winced and looked away for a long moment. Finally, she touched my cheek and said, 'Lights out.'

As my mum's footsteps retreated down the hallway, I lay on my stomach - the only position that provided any comfort – and closed my eyes, but I couldn't sleep. My mind was racing. It was at that moment that I realised something I should probably have realised much sooner. Bill, with his straight, sandy hair, looked nothing like me. Neither did any of my siblings. Jane's hair was red. And yet mine was dark and curly. I was tall for my age, and thin, while they were all short and round. I was their 'gift'. But I was not one of them, and never would be.

That night, I dreamt about my 'real' mother and father. In my dream, I could see neither of their faces, but I knew that they cared … that they were searching for me. I woke up to feel the loss of them. It was a loss I felt even more acutely as I walked downstairs to sit at the dining table, opposite my supposed brother and sisters, my make-believe parents. As the backs of my legs met the chair, pain shot through me but I didn't make a sound. As I filled my bowl with cornflakes, I could sense Jane watching me with concern, but I avoided her gaze.

For several months after Bill gave me the strap, life in the house returned to the way it had been before then. I was still grateful for the things I had – the clothes, the toys, the food and of course my own bedroom - but I needed more. I desperately wanted to have a parent pick me up and cuddle me, to tickle me, to tell me I was loved. I had seen other families showing this sort of affection at the park and at school. I had even seen Bill and Jane behave this way towards my siblings.

One afternoon, while watching my favourite cartoon, *Fantastic Four*, I overheard Jane and Bill having a heated but hushed conversation in the kitchen. 'He's out,' Jane whispered. 'And he's looking for his children.' Immediately, I knew that my suspicions had been correct. Whoever *he* was must be looking for me. I went to bed that night and took comfort in the fact that this might not actually be the life I was meant to be living. The people who loved me might be searching for me right now.

As the summer holidays ended and the February days grew even hotter with the sort of heat that doesn't fade with the sun and is still there to greet you the next morning, I attended my first day of school. Jane walked me to the gate, where the other parents stood, kissing and waving goodbye to tiny children in blue and grey uniforms. Some of the kids were excited, some nervous, some crying. Some of the mothers were crying, too, but tried not to show it. I held out my arms for a hug, and Jane patted me on the head. 'Be a good boy,' she said.

'I will,' I said.

'I will what?' she asked, her voice quiet but firm.

'I will, Mummy.'

I made my way to the classroom door. When I looked back, Jane was gone.

Although I was not yet five, I was an accomplished reader and enjoyed class, as well as having people to play with. Over the weeks that followed, I learned to take pride in my work, including writing my name on one line, the capital P at the start reaching through the perforated line to the solid line above.

My teacher's name was Miss Harris. She was young and always seemed excited to see us.

At school, I laughed a lot; at home, I did not. At school, I could say and even do silly things and not get in trouble.

One day, as the other kids were heading out to recess, Miss Harris called me over and told me that she had noticed I wasn't smiling or laughing as much as normal. 'Is everything okay, Peter?' She asked.

I nodded.

'Are you tired?' she asked.

I nodded again.

She made a sympathetic face, her bottom lip jutting out. 'You're not getting enough sleep?'

'No. I can't. I need to wait.'

Now, she looked puzzled. 'Wait for what, Peter?'

'For my real family to come and get me,' I explained.

Miss Harris gave me a quick, warm hug, and told me that the hard times pass and there are always better days ahead. She walked me by the hand to the classroom door and told me to have fun. I ran off in the direction of the playground and my favourite equipment, the monkey bars. When I looked back, she was still watching. My heart felt suddenly full and my mood lifted.

It was on a dreary Sunday morning that my life would change forever. We hadn't been to Church yet, so it must have been early. Jane was in the garden, clipping flowers from her rose bushes. I was running from one end of the yard to the other, counting out loud as I ran each 'lap', trying to beat my previous score.

The front gate squeaked as it opened and two people entered, walking towards Jane. One was a woman, well-dressed and official-looking. The other was a man of medium height with thick, muscular arms and dark hair. He wasn't approaching Jane; he was approaching me. He wore the biggest smile I had ever seen. As I watched in silence, he dropped to one knee on the grass in front of me, his blue eyes brimming with tears. 'Pete,' he said.

'He's out. And he's looking for his children.'

At that moment, I remembered my dream: my mum and dad, searching for me. Wanting to bring me home. Finally, the man in the dream had a face.

Without a word, the man put his arms out and I leapt into them. I held him so tight my arms hurt. He held me for a long time. Then he pulled back slightly, and regarded me with his blue eyes, saying, 'Do you remember me?'

Through trembling lips, I mumbled, 'Can we go home, Dad?'

Minutes later, Dad – my *real* dad – carried me out the front gate of the house I had occupied for the last three years, heading towards a waiting station wagon. As we got closer, I heard the sound of excited voices, and saw two girls sitting in the back seat, their faces pressed against the glass. One looked two or three years older than me, the other another two or three years older still. Both were thin, with curly brown hair. They were cheering.

# Chapter 3

# HOMECOMING

As the car pulled away from the kerb, the two girls in the back seat – *my sisters*, I told myself, in disbelief - introduced themselves. 'I'm Tina,' the older one said. She was very well-spoken, loud and confident, and I knew she would be bossy. She had long, dark hair. The girl beside her had short hair and wore a slightly startled expression that made me like her immediately. 'That's Kelly,' Tina said.

As we drove away from the Robinsons' house in the suburbs and through the outskirts of the city, Tina talked non-stop. She told me about her school, where she had to wear a uniform and seemed to have an endless list of friends. Kelly kept watching me, her big brown eyes wide open. I didn't say much. I just listened. It was a strange feeling to be travelling in a car with my family, none of whom I could remember, but I was happy. As the city buildings came into sight, I asked Dad where we were going.

'Home,' he said and flashed me a grin.

Finally, we passed a sign that read Welcome to Willoughby and, a little while later, we pulled into a single concrete driveway that lead to a neat brick house. There were a few small patches of greeny-yellow grass in the front yard, but it was mostly dirt.

My sisters were excited to get me out of the car and show me to my room. They pulled me up the front path, down the dark, narrow hallway, and into a bedroom at the rear of the house. As I passed by their room, I noticed that it looked *lived in,* and wondered how long they had been together before they came to find me.

My room was small, furnished only with a single bed, but I instantly felt it was where I belonged. I was unpacking when Dad called for us, and we ran to the loungeroom. He sat on the sofa, holding a packet of Tim Tams. He handed one to each of us. I had never had one before and remember forcing myself to eat it slowly, even when the milk chocolate melted all over my fingers. As I ate, I watched how the girls ate theirs. For Kelly, the Tim Tam was gone in three bites, while Tina prised apart the two biscuits within, licked the creamy centre, then ate the biscuits in measured bites.

I had finished my biscuit and was hungrily eyeing the rest of the packet when Tina said, 'Dad stole me from school, you know.' She looked proud. 'And the cops came and found us.'

'That's not exactly right, Tina,' Dad said. He offered each of us another biscuit. I took it and began the same slow process of nibbling at one end.

Over the next half hour, Dad explained what had happened to each of us since the day Pop took us to church to be adopted. For the first time, I heard how Tina, Kelly and I had been taken in by separate families, while Dave had been allowed to stay with our grandparents. I asked why they decided to keep him, and Dad shrugged. I asked whether he was going to come and live with us, and Dad shook his head. 'Not right now,' he said. Dad told me that Dave used to save his pocket money and call Dad, in jail, every Friday from a phone box near school. After Dad got out, he showed up at Dave's school and told him he was going to find all the kids, but Dave said he didn't want to leave his Nan.

I could see how sad this made Dad, and wanted to give him a hug, but I held back, nervous that he might not return the gesture.

By pure coincidence, it was when he visited Dave's primary school that Dad spotted Tina. She was playing in the quadrangle. 'Isn't that your sister?' he asked. Dave nodded. Apparently, she had been given to another Seventh Day Adventist Church family, who had unknowingly sent her to the same school as Dave. Half an hour later, police swarmed the tiny campus and local intersections and roads were locked down. Tina was missing, presumed kidnapped. By early afternoon, there was a manhunt operation in place to find the offender.

Eventually they found Dad and Tina. Dad was arrested, and Tina was returned to the family that had raised her for the last several years. In jail that night, Dad realised he'd have to do things 'by the book'. The next morning, he'd called a lawyer and begun the hard work of retrieving the three of us legally. This took more than 18 months. Dad laughed when he told us how surprised the judge looked that he wanted full custody of his kids, a foreign concept to most men in those days.

I listened carefully, but I didn't really understand what my dad was telling me. The only thing I knew for sure was that it wasn't fair that a parent would have to steal their own kids back. I told Dad that's how I felt, and he mussed my hair affectionately. 'You're a smart boy, Pete,' he said, his voice a little husky.

For the next few weeks, I spent every minute of the day with my sisters. It was like discovering new friends in the playground, but we went home together at the end of the day. Like me, my sisters had developed their own survival strategies in the years we'd spent apart. Tina continued to dominate every conversation and situation; she told us what games we would play and made the rules up as she went. Kelly had an amazing ability to just roll with whatever Tina said and acted as peacemaker on the odd occasion that Tina and I disagreed. For my part, I had learned to watch and listen.

It was when we were playing spotlight one evening, and Tina was searching for us, that Kelly told me what it had been like for her during the years we were apart. In halting whispers, as Tina got closer and then then further away, Kelly told me about the couple who had taken her in.

Unlike the family that took me, the Johnsons had no children of their own. She had only been living with them for a few months when they told her they were going to go on a plane ride, to Queensland, where they had bought a new house for the three of them. The house was red brick, with a horseshoe-shaped driveway, and led onto two acres of rolling green grass. For her birthday that year, the Johnsons gave Kelly a beautiful pony, chestnut with a white diamond on its forehead. She was riding the pony the day her real Dad arrived.

Unlike me, Kelly hadn't wanted to leave her adoptive family, but she had no choice. With tears in his eyes, Mr Johnson explained that this man was her real father. Kelly told me that she cried as they drove away from her family, her house, her horse, and it had been days before she said a word to Dad. Since coming to live with her, I had often found Kelly playing in the backyard alone, just sitting watching ants or chasing butterflies. Now I thought about her riding her horse and realised that her life might have been even harder than mine.

A couple of months after we arrived in Willoughby, it was time to leave again. Dad didn't tell us why, but there was no rush. We had plenty of time to pack our bags, and the girls even got a chance to say goodbye to their friends and teachers. I hadn't been to school yet, so I spent the day before we left helping Dad clean the house. As we drove away from the little brick house, I felt only a slight pang of remorse: it didn't matter where we lived so long as the four of us were together.

Our next house was more basic than the last – smaller, with chipped lino floor in the kitchen and a tiny toilet that always smelled. I went to the local school, and was surprised when another boy teased me for living in a commission house. I said I didn't live in a commission place, but he insisted, so that night I asked Dad whether this was true, and he told me it was. He was slightly red-faced, from embarrassment rather than anger, when he explained that it wasn't easy to find a good job when you'd been 'inside'. I think that must have been the first time he actually said the word, but of course the girls had told me he'd been in prison. They didn't know how many times, and I didn't ask Dad.

While we went to school, Dad worked whenever and wherever he could, doing odd jobs including cleaning, none of which seemed to pay very much. It was hard for him to find something with regular work hours because he had to drop us off and pick us up from school.

Despite having my own bedroom, I spent every night in Dad's bed, cuddled up against his warm, hairy shoulder. Sometimes, my hand would find his during the night, and we would still be holding hands in the morning.

It was only because I slept in his bed that I knew how often Dad left the house at night. At least a couple of times each week, he would go out for hours, returning just before the girls awoke. Instinctively, I knew not to ask where he went. I knew, too, not to ask why nice bikes would suddenly appear in the house, or why we were not allowed to ride them in the street. I knew to not ask why one week we had a brand-new TV which was gone a week later, only to be replaced by another new one in time for the *The Wonderful World of Disney* on a Sunday evening.

Dad didn't seem to have many friends at this time, although there were a few who showed up now and then. One was a tall, thin, clean-shaven man with mutton chop sideburns and low, dark eyebrows. My dad introduced him as 'Coxy'. It was only when I researched Dad's life many years later that I realised who

Coxy really was: 'Mad Dog' Russell Cox, one of Australia's most notorious criminals. He and Dad, I discovered, were incarcerated at Tamworth Boys' Home in the mid-1950s, an institution designed to house boys who had escaped from other institutions. Walking through Tamworth's doors meant being flogged by the guards, who wanted to let every new inmate know who was boss. Dad never mentioned it to me, which I think is the best indication of how horrible it must have been.

Coxy would visit late at night, long after my sisters had gone to bed and I was meant to be asleep. Then he and Dad would sit in the kitchen, drinking tins of VB and speaking in hushed tones. Quite often there was another man who would turn-up at the same time; Dad called him Wombat. He was always kind to us kids, bringing small gifts or bags of lollies and leaving them on the bench for us to find after he left. Sometimes, when I woke up early, one or both Coxy and Wombat would be asleep in the living room.

One evening, we were watching the news. Kelly and I were sitting on Dad's lap, while Tina curled up on the couch beside us. The crime report focused on a man who had been stopped at a traffic light in downtown Sydney when a gunman shot him in the back of the head. Then the screen changed to show a photograph of the victim's smiling face. It was Wombat. Shocked, I looked at

Dad, awaiting his reaction, but his face remained calm. He never mentioned Wombat again.

Occasionally, we would climb into the Holden and Dad would drive us to visit Dave. He would wait in the pub for a couple of hours while we played cricket against the large, dilapidated stables, or chased my grandparents' dog.

On one of these visits, Dave found me looking at a photograph of Mum in the living room. She had shiny blond hair, flushed cheeks and a crooked smile. 'Do you remember her?' Dave asked.

'Nope. You?'

'Yes.'

'Do you know where she is?' I asked.

He shook his head.

'Does anyone?'

Dave shrugged, then said, 'Come on! Wanna help clean my gun?'

I ran after him. As we cleaned and polished the air rifle, I asked Dave whether he really preferred living with Nan and Pop to living with us.

'Most of the time,' Dave said. Then he confided that, when he misbehaved, Pop would threaten to take him to the orphanage. Although I'd heard parents at school and in the park make the same threat many times, I could see how much it scared Dave.

As we headed back outside, it struck me how strange and painful it must have been the first day he returned to our grandparents' house without his siblings. The big old place must have seemed so quiet.

As we restarted our cricket game, Dave asked, 'What's Dad like?' He bowled the ball.

I swung my bat, catching the edge of the ball, causing it to fly into thick scrub under a sprawling fig tree. As I searched for the ball, I tried to think of how to answer Dave's question, but I couldn't. Finally locating the ball, I handed it to him with a shrug. 'He's okay, I guess,' I said.

'Is he rough with you?'

I told Dave that Dad was fairer than my adoptive father had been, but when he hit me, it was the same: a strap against the backs of my bare legs.

'Shit,' Dave said.

'Gotta be cruel to be kind,' I answered. One of Dad's favourite sayings.

It was after we returned home from Dural one evening that everything changed once more. Tina's birthday was only a couple of weeks away, and she was convinced that Dad had a present for her hidden somewhere in the house. While he took a nap in the living room, Tina, Kelly and I searched the whole house as quietly as we could. We had found nothing, and were preparing to give up our search, when I remembered the top of Dad's wardrobe. I had seen him put something up there after he'd returned home early one morning.

Quietly, we took a chair from the kitchen, and I volunteered to climb on it, because I was the tallest. Despite my height, I had to stand on my toes and stretch my fingers as far as they would reach before I touched something. It was plastic. A bag, I figured. Grasping the edge of the plastic with my fingers, I pulled it towards me, and just managed to catch it as it fell from the wardrobe.

I placed the bag on the bed, and the three of us opened it together. We gasped. Inside were bundles of cash, neatly bound with thick red elastic bands. And there were three handguns, like the ones cops and robbers had on TV.

With a loud yawn, Dad stirred. The couch creaked as he sat up, and he called out, 'Kids? Where are you?'

I picked up the bag and wrapped it up the best I could, then climbed back onto the chair. It wobbled as I put the plastic bag back where I'd found it. As we ran back to the kitchen and replaced the chair under the table, Dad came out of the living room, stretching. 'Sorry,' he said, 'Must've nodded off.' We must have looked guilty, because he said, 'Something wrong?'

I froze. I couldn't lie to him. I didn't have to.

'Nope,' Tina said, her voice confident. 'What's for dinner, Dad?'

As Tina and Dad scoured the pantry, I glanced at Kelly. She looked as scared as I felt. I knew right then than none of us would ever mention the money or guns again.

Later that night, Dad woke me up by shaking my shoulder. I had no idea what time it was, but I knew it was late. I winced as Dad snapped on the light. 'Get up, Pete!' he said, his voice sharp. 'Pack your things. You've got two minutes.' Then he was gone, and I could hear him telling the girls the same thing.

Several times over the last couple of months, Dad had told us that we might have to leave in a hurry one day. He had told us to think about what we would take and what we would leave behind. I placed Tom the Turtle gently into my bag, along with a few items of clothing. Then, thinking that Tom might not be able to breathe in the bag, I unzipped it a little and pulled his head out.

When I turned around, I saw Dad reaching for the top of the wardrobe and heard the rustle of plastic. Then he was stuffing the plastic bag into a large black rucksack.

Wiping sweat from his forehead, Dad gave me a tense smile. 'You ready, Pete?' he asked.

'Yes, Dad,' I said.

'That's my boy.'

## Chapter 4

# NEW PLACES, NEW PROMISES

According to the dashboard clock, it was a little after 4am when Kelly and Tina joined me in the car. They looked tired and confused. None of us spoke. My heart was racing. Was someone coming for us?

Dad tossed the last of our stuff in the boot and climbed into the car, then accelerated quickly out of the driveway and roads that, by day, were normally bustling with traffic. At this time of the morning, they were eerily quiet. As we passed the milk bar that we'd visited many times to spend ten or twenty cents worth of lollies, Dad looked across at me. Then he put a hand on the back of my head, rubbing his thumb gently back and forth. Usually, his touch would have soothed me. Now, it just made me feel more nervous. I forced a smile, then turned to look out the window, watching the orange streetlights flick past.

We drove for what seemed like at least an hour, my eyes occasionally closing and sleep taking over before I would snap awake again and remember what was happening. Finally, Dad turned into the parking lot of a motel, its large, neon sign advertising colour TVs in every room. He pulled the car to a stop and opened his door. 'Back in a sec,' he said.

I watched Dad climb out of the car, then I looked over my shoulder at the girls. They were both asleep, leaning inwards towards each other as far as their seatbelts would allow.

Through the front window of the reception office, I watched Dad walk up to the desk and tap a small silver bell. I couldn't hear it from this distance, but I imagined the tinny *ding ding*. He waited a minute or more. When nobody appeared, he rang again. Finally, a middle-aged man with messy hair and dishevelled clothing appeared from a room in the back. He looked peeved at being woken up and rubbed red, swollen eyes as Dad counted out his cash. Then he retrieved a key from beneath the desk and handed it to Dad.

A minute later, Dad pulled our car into the parking spot directly in front of our door, and I followed him into our room. The girls were behind me, both shuffling their feet, barely awake. The room smelled clean and fresh and the two double beds looked inviting. The two girls shared one while, as usual, I climbed in next to Dad.

I woke sometime later to the sound of the kettle squealing. When I opened my eyes, sunlight was streaming through the gauzy curtains. Despite the noise of the kettle, neither of the girls had woken up. Dad gave me a smile and put a finger to his lips, indicating that I should let them sleep. Then he sat on the edge of the bed to drink his coffee. As the rich warm smell of Blend 43 washed over me, I lay down again and realised that I could be happy anywhere, so long as we were together.

For the next four days and nights, us kids stayed in the motel room, even when Dad went out. I was desperate to run around but knew there must be a good reason why he wanted us to stay inside. He only left at night, returning after twenty minutes with grocery items purchased from a petrol station down the block. I remember eating cereal out of the box and cooking two-minute noodles in the kettle. If we were well-behaved all day, we received a chocolate bar. Mars and Snickers were my favourites.

On the fifth day, Dad got up early in the morning, the streetlights still visible through the curtains. I watched his blue-grey form slip out of bed. A moment later, he was barely visible against the black oblong of the open door. Then I got out of bed and watched at the window as he jogged across the carpark and the narrow road to a public phone box. He made a single call, speaking for less than a minute. When he came back, I pretended to be asleep. Then I must have really slept, because the next thing

I remember is waking up to see Kelly and Tina up and dressed. Dad was smiling. As I sat up, he wrapped an arm around me and said, 'I was just telling your sisters we've got a place to stay!'

Beaming, he explained that he'd found us a a house on the other side of Sydney, in the suburb of Claymore. His enthusiasm was infectious. We quickly ate breakfast, and us kids were laughing and playfighting by the time we jumped into the car.

Our new house was a two-storey semi-detached, part of a newly established court of perfectly aligned housing commission homes. Our place was the first on the left as we entered the court. This meant that we had a view of the local primary school. 'That's Badgally Primary,' Dad said. 'You'll be starting there next week.'

As he had promised, the following week, Tina, Kelly and I showed up for our first day. I never asked whether the girls liked their class, but I liked mine. We quickly settled into a routine. One of the benefits of moving so often was that we had developed the ability to make friends easily. After spending the hours 9 to 330 at school, we would return home only to spend the next four hours playing with several other kids who lived in our street. I can't remember any of their names today.

Around three weeks after we had started at the school, I was sitting in class when I saw my dad walking down the hallway outside the classroom, accompanied by the school principal. I was nervous all day, wondering whether Tina, Kelly or I were in trouble, but when we got home that afternoon, he told us he'd successfully applied for the job of cleaner.

When other kids saw Dad wearing grey overalls and sweeping up or – worse yet - emptying the bins, they nudged each other or said things under their breath. Despite this, I never felt embarrassed for him. I felt proud. Each day, when we came home, we would find him sitting in the front room, reading the paper and drinking strong milky tea, and he would spend a few minutes asking each of us about our day. For a little while at least, he seemed like a different man to the one who had once hidden money and guns on top of his wardrobe ... whose friends were killed in the streets.

When he wasn't working at the school, Dad picked up other odd jobs around the neighbourhood. After doing some some gardening and maintenance for an elderly couple, he returned with a bike that had belonged to their grandson. When I arrived home from school, the bike was sitting in the lounge room. It wasn't just any bike. It was a blue and yellow Raleigh BMX! The kind of bike that kids who said mean things about Dad's job would envy. I was instantly in love. For the next hour, Dad and I washed and polished the chrome frame until it gleamed.

From that day on, I was up before 6am, waiting on the front lawn, my BMX proudly leaning on its kickstand while I waited for Dad to wake up and give me 20c to buy the Sydney Morning Herald. Cruising down to the milk bar as the streetlights turned off and the sky changed from pink to blue was the best part of my day. With so many early morning trips to the newsagent, it wasn't long before I was offered my first job: delivering papers around the surrounding twenty blocks. I asked Dad whether I could do it and he said yes – that it would be a good way for me to develop my sense of responsibility – so I accepted. I spent each morning riding around my paper route, feeling the cool breeze on my cheeks, and the satisfaction of developing the perfect throw. I didn't even mind when it rained; in fact, I liked the challenge of navigating the slick streets and keeping each plastic-wrapped paper under cover until just before I had to toss it. For the first time, I knew what it meant to take pride in your work. I also enjoyed seeing the neighbourhood come to life every morning, the same cars switching on their headlights and backing out of driveways, the same people giving me a wave as we passed.

I always rode carefully, keeping close to the curb like Dad had told me watching out for turning cars or those that came close alongside me. I never even came *close* to having an accident until I'd been delivering papers for three weeks. That morning was otherwise unremarkable. It was a little cold, so my breath formed clouds in front of me as I pedalled. I was around three blocks from home and had just reached into my satchel, ready to toss my next newspaper, but I never did.

The next thing I was aware of was three strangers staring down at me. I was no longer outside. The figures were backlit by a fluorescent bulb. So I wasn't outside. But I wasn't in hospital either. This was a regular house. We had light fixtures just like those.

'Dad?' I said, groggily.

'You've had a bit of an accident,' a woman said, leaning down and touching my hair with gentle fingers. 'We found you lying in the gutter and brought you back to our place. An ambulance is on the way.'

Then one of the other people stepped forward and I felt a cold, sharp pain spread across my top lip. 'It's just ice,' a man's voice said. Now, he came into focus. Like the woman, he wore a look of concern.

I tried to ask where Dad was, but I must have passed out, because the next thing I knew, there were uniformed people in the room. They told me they were paramedics. They asked me my name. I managed to tell them it was Peter. Then they asked whether I knew what had happened.

'An ... an accident,' I mumbled, remembering what the woman had told me.

'Good,' one of the paramedics said. He had introduced himself as Dan. 'Very good.'

Suddenly, there was a commotion and I recognised Dad's voice calling my name. Immediately, I started to cry, then felt ashamed until I saw the tears on his cheeks as well. He rode in the ambulance with me, holding my hand. Suddenly, I felt surprisingly calm.

As the ambulance jostled back and forth and the siren wailed, I listened to Dad and the paramedic talking. In my groggy state, I had imagined that I had been hit by a car. Apparently not. According to a woman who had been walking past at the time, my front wheel had hit some building refuse in the gutter and I had been catapulted over the handlebars, before landing directly on a builder's brick. My top lip had had been torn away from the left corner of my mouth, which explained why I was having so much trouble speaking. Despite the pain, I wanted desperately to know what had happened to my bike.

As soon as we arrived at the hospital, I was rushed in to see a plastic surgeon, who assured me I would be okay. Then a nurse put a mask over my face, doing her best to make the seal tight while not touching my torn lip, and I felt sleep rushing towards me. I spent the next three hours in surgery as the plastic surgeon did his best to reattach my upper lip. Then I was wheeled into a room that I would share with three other boys.

At some point that evening, I woke up briefly, crying out due to the pain. A nurse brought me a syringe full of liquid that she helped me to swallow, and I fell asleep again.

The next morning, I woke up feeling hungry and tried to eat a bowl of jelly, but it was impossible. I tried some ice-cream with more success the freezing strawberry mouthfuls numbed my mouth. Over the next few days, as my lip began to mend, I was able to eat a whole bowl of jelly without crying from the pain.

My bike's frame, I later found out, was completely warped. I asked Dad whether we could get it fixed, and he said we'd have to see, but I already knew from his tone that the answer was no. And no bike meant no paper route.

Dad never blamed me for the accident, but I blamed myself. Because of this, the days I spent in hospital were some of the loneliest of my life.

When I returned home, the place felt different somehow. Dad was still there before and after school, he still did his janitorial work during the day and the occasional odd jobs for people around the neighbourhood when they required, but he no longer seemed as content as he had when we first moved in. Now, instead of reading the paper in the afternoon when we returned from school, he would just sit and stare out the window. I knew something was wrong, but I didn't know what it was.

It was one day, as I stared into the empty shelves of the fridge, that it finally clicked. It had been a long time since we'd had fish and chips for tea, or our favourite breakfast cereal. Sometimes there was no milk, so we had to eat our Weet-bix dry. I knew instinctively what this meant, but I never complained. None of us did.

One Saturday morning, Dad told us to get in the car and drove us to a nearby branch of the Smith Family. We were interviewed by an old woman with a kind face, who filled out some forms and then invited the four of us into a back room. She handed us each a bag of clean clothes, neatly folded. Then she took us into another room, which was lined with shelves of food, just like a tiny supermarket. She gave us a small trolley and told Dad he could fill it up.

I watched Dad select the cans and packets of food with great care. He favoured rice and pasta, which was fine with me. I tried putting a box of Coco Pops in the trolley, but Dad just shook his head and I returned the box to the shelf without protest. When we were finished shopping, I expected Dad to pay, but the old woman waved us on and we just left.

Moments later, we placed our bags of food and clothing in the boot. Dad drove home in silence, his cheeks red, his jaw tight. I didn't really understand what was wrong, but I knew better than to ask.

I could have coped with not getting treats or my favourite cereal. All of us could. But Dad couldn't let it go. Over the next few weeks, I heard him slam the fridge door on a few occasions, and when Tina found some mould on a slice of bread, he threw away the whole loaf, including the toast I was eating, then dropped the dishes into the sink with a clatter. He didn't joke around with us anymore and I found myself missing him even when he was right there.

Clearly, we needed money. That's what gave me my Big Idea. It was a wet Saturday morning and I'd been woken up by Dad swearing as he spilled his cup of home brand instant coffee. I went into the girls' room and told them we needed to talk.

'Where?' Tina asked.

'Cubby,' I said.

There was a small storage area underneath the house. It could be accessed by a small door. I'd seen in the day we moved in and had climbed in a few times when I needed to cry without anybody seeing. Kelly didn't like it because of the spider webs, but I told her she would be okay and she gave me a brave nod.

In hushed tones, I told the girls my plan. I hadn't been sure how sensible it was, but they seemed to think it was a good idea. Feeling encouraged, I suggested we shake on it, which we all did. Then we crawled back out from under the house, dusted ourselves off, and headed back inside.

Because she was the oldest, Tina took responsibility for setting the plan in motion. It was her job to tell Dad that we were going to meet up with friends. Instead, we walked four blocks to Claymore High School. I had ridden my bike over there a few times, so I knew the school grounds quite well, and I knew that nobody would be there on the weekend. My plan was to break in, find anything worth stealing, then sell it to help Dad buy some real groceries.

For a few moments, we stood outside the school's back door. I picked up a large stone and threw it as hard as I could at the glass near the handle. It shattered, leaving sharp shards protruding from the timber frame. I carefully reached in through the gap, my thin arm missing the shards by millimetres as I found the lock with the tips of my fingers. I twisted the latch, then pushed the door open with a flourish.

It was a large school, with a central hub that connected all wings of the building. We began our search in the teachers' offices, searching through desk draws. In some we found money

- mostly loose change - which we put in our pockets. In others, there were watches and personal belongings, which we also took. We found a staff room with a large central table, upon which sat a small tin with a picture of the children's hospital on the side. Seeing a picture of that building, which was so familiar to me, gave me a moment's pause. Then we emptied it out, watching coins spill out across the table.

Next, the girls decided to check one of the classrooms. I had noticed a large sliding door that looked as though it led to the central hub of the main building. With the success we'd had so far, I was feeling confident and told Tina and Kelly that I was going to head into another section. I made my way along a locker-lined hallway and placed all my bodyweight against the door at the end. Finally, it creaked open, revealing another hall that was much darker than the one in which I stood.

For a moment, I paused. I didn't want to turn back and have to admit to the girls that I was scared. But they might *not* make fun of me. They might even offer to come with me.

I was just about to pull the door shut when I heard a footstep behind me. I whirled around and a man grabbed me by my collar, lifting me up with his other arm. I tried to scream, but he clapped a hand over my mouth.

The man carried me down the hall, through the atrium, and into one of the classrooms, where Tina and Kelly had found another coin purse. Hearing our approach and assuming it was just me, Tina turned around with a smile. Then she saw me tucked under the big man's arm and screamed.

As he held me off the ground, I heard my heart pulsing in my ears. I wanted to scream, too, but my voice wouldn't work. Then he dropped me on the ground and pushed me roughly in Tina's direction. She caught me and held me against her. I could feel her shaking. Beside us, Kelly was crying silently.

'Alright, that's enough blubbering,' the man said.

Now that I could see him from a distance, I realised he wore a uniform, but he didn't look like a police officer. This uniform wasn't blue, it was grey, with a shield emblem sewn on to his shirt pocket. It read SECURITY.

Positioned between the three of us and the classroom door, the security guard pulled a chair out from beneath one of the desks and sat down. He leaned forward, his stomach hanging well past his belt. He was red-faced and sweating. Removing a small notepad and pen from his pants' pocket, he raised his eyebrows. 'Go on, then,' he said. 'Give us your names.'

It was at this moment that I felt – rather than saw - Tina's stance change. She had stopped shaking and stood a little taller. Then she reached out and placed a hand lightly on Kelly's shoulder. 'I'm Tracy Peters,' she said, her tone confident. 'This is my sister Cathy, and my brother, Steven.'

The guard nodded as he wrote down these names. 'And your address?' he asked.

Tina reeled off a completely fictional location.

As my terror began to subside, I felt my admiration for Tina grow. There was something about the way she was speaking – not just the words, but her tone - that made me think of Dad … the way he spoke sometimes, as if he was completely *sure* of something when I knew for a fact that he couldn't be.

As the security guard continued to write, Tina looked down at me. Then she looked back towards the security guard and gave an almost imperceptible jerk of her head, indicating – with her chin – the open door behind him. I looked at Kelly. She had stopped crying now and gave me a tiny nod.

'Please, sir,' Tina said, 'Don't tell our mum what we did!'

The guard glanced up, shook his head and snorted with contempt. Then he went back to writing. As he flipped his notepad page, we began to run. Kelly, then me, then Tina. The guard should simply have reached out and grabbed one of us, but he miscalculated. He tried to get up first, and the extra second it took allowed us to get past him. Then we were in the hallway, our runners pounding the linoleum as we ran towards the atrium.

By the time we reached the school's front door, I was in front. I stopped, opening it for my sisters. The guard was running down the hallway, only four metres from where I stood. I waited for Tina, then stepped through the doorway and pulled the door shut, buying us another second or two. And we were off, running again, our legs stretching out ahead of us as we dashed across the oval.

Finally, I looked back. At first the guard looked like he might keep running, propelled by his anger and humiliation at being bested by three children, but after ten or twenty metres he gave up, hunched over, hands on his knees.

I laughed. Then Tina and Kelly were laughing too. We scaled the high wire fence and dropped onto the other side, giggling hysterically, while the security guard shouted something far behind us.

When we got home, Dad was sitting in the kitchen, listening to the horse racing. He had the same look he always had when we listened to the races: a thoughtful frown, his eyes bright and hopeful. As we entered the kitchen, I paused a moment, wondering whether we should tell him what happened. Dad had always told us we wouldn't get into trouble so long as we told the truth.

I was still wondering whether this was the right approach when Tina stepped past me and started pulling handfuls of coins, watches, and other trinkets out of her pockets. She dropped them on the kitchen table so that Dad could see them. Then Kelly did the same, and I followed.

Dad was no longer listening to the races. We had his full attention. For a few moments, he said nothing. Then his frown deepened and his eyes lost their joy. 'Where the Hell did all of this come from?' he roared.

I jumped. We all did. We'd never seen Dad look so angry. Suddenly, I was more scared than I had been when the guard grabbed me.

It was *my* idea. I knew that it was my responsibility to explain it. 'I'm sorry,' I said, then took a deep, shaky breath before I continued. '[We … we broke into the high school and stole these things.' When he glowered at me, I whimpered, 'We … we just wanted you to be happy again.'

Finally, Dad's expression softened, and for a moment I thought I saw tears welling in his eyes. Then his look hardened and he motioned for us to sit at the kitchen table in front of him.

For the next fifteen minutes, Dad made us tell him everything. He wanted to know exactly how we got into the school, how we were caught, how we escaped. While we spoke – our voices overlapping - he listened intently. Then he used the blade of his palm to make our haul into a pile in the middle of the table and placed everything into an empty margarine container.

I listened to Dad's footsteps as he walked up the hallway, then I heard the floor creak and imagined him standing on his toes to place the container on top of his wardrobe. I still wasn't sure how bad the punishment would be, but that we would be punished I had no doubt. When he returned to the kitchen, I felt him touch my hair, and winced. Then I realised that he was tousling my hair.

'Who wants a cup of tea?' Dad said.

We all nodded sheepishly.

As Dad turned away to fill the kettle, I realised something remarkable: he was no longer mad. He was proud. Even if he wouldn't say so.

I was six years old and I had just performed my first break-and-entry. It wouldn't be my last.

# Chapter 5

# LESSONS IN DISHONESTY

My second break-in was closer to home. Right next door, in fact, at Badgally Primary School. Access would be easier, thanks to Dad's Maintenance keys, which we'd taken from the top drawer of his bedside cabinet. This time, we had another accomplice: Gavin, a kid from the grade above mine. We broke in early one evening, after the last of the teachers had gone home and while Dad was still out.

We entered the school through a door that was usually reserved for the Grade 2 students; it meant that we could get in and out without being seen from the street in front of the school. Then we ran through the grade 2 classroom and into the main hall. It felt so strange to be in the place after hours. In the Art room, we searched the teacher's desk, rifling through paperclips and detention slips, but found only a few coins. I was pocketing these when Gavin yelled, 'Hey, guys, watch this!' While we'd been searching for valuables, he had been laying plastic paint containers on the ground. Now, he was unscrewing their lids. As we watched, he lay each on its side, then took a run-up and jumped on the first one. Blue paint spurted halfway across the room. Delighted, he jumped on the next and the next, adding green and yellow to the mess.

My mouth hung open. I looked at my sisters and saw the shock on their faces. I knew we were thinking the same thing: Dad would have to clean this up.

Minutes later, we were leaving by the door to the grade 2 classroom. Gavin hadn't understood why we didn't want to join in on the vandalism, or why we wanted to leave so soon. At first, he pleaded with us. Then he got angry. As we left the school by the front gate, making sure that nobody saw us, Gavin called us babies and ran down the street in the direction of his home. We only had to walk next door and duck inside.

Tina put the keys back in Dad's bedroom drawer. Then we made milo and sat in front of the TV until we heard dad's car pull up in the driveway, its suspension creaking as he climbed out. As we heard the front door open, I looked at my sisters and realised that none of us had said a word since we got home.

It was when Dad called out, 'Hey there! Why are you sitting in the dark?' that I saw my white volleys where I'd kicked them off and felt my stomach sink. There were green splotches on them.

I didn't know whether the paint had splashed my runners when Gavin jumped on the container or as we ran across the classroom afterwards, but there it was: proof that we'd been there. Even from across the room, I felt like I could smell the paint. And I knew there would be no hiding it from Dad.

He stepped into the room and switched on the light. For a moment, he looked like he was about to say something – maybe something teasing, something about watching too much TV or something. Then he saw our faces and his smile faded. 'What is it?' he asked.

Before either of the others could say anything, I told Dad exactly what had happened. As I spoke, I watched his face get redder and redder and knew that something bad was coming. Then I finished and he told me to stand up and walk to him. I did so. He looked down at me, his expression grim, then squeezed my shoulder.

'I'm glad you told me, mate,' he said. It was the first time he'd called me mate. I had to resist the urge to burst into tears.

'You know this was the wrong thing to do, don't you?' he asked.

I nodded. As he glanced at my sisters above my head, I knew that they, too, would be nodding.

A moment later, Dad left the room. The next time I saw him, he was wearing his grey overalls and carrying his keys. He left the house without a word.

Tina made the three of us macaroni and cheese from a packet, which we usually enjoyed, but neither Kelly nor I had much of an appetite. We ate at the kitchen table, then tipped most of the stodgy mixture into the bin and went to our bedrooms. I tried reading a comic, but I couldn't concentrate.

I was asleep when I heard Dad come home. I listened to the sound of him shrugging off his coarse overalls. Then he tossed them in the washing machine and turned the dial. There was a loud click as the machine came on. I heard the rhythmic tink-tink, tink-tink of buttons as the drum spun. Then Dad switched on the kettle and I fell asleep once more.

The next morning, I found my volleys on the end of my bed. Dad had scrubbed them and used shoe whitener to disguise the green paint on them, but I knew that I would never enjoy wearing the shoes again. Before I left for school, Dad repeated what he'd said the night before. 'You did the right thing, telling me the truth,' he said. 'But you know I've gotta punish you.'

I nodded, knowing that the anticipation of the belt across my legs as I sat in school all day would be worse than the punishment when it eventually came.

That day, my final class was in the art room. As I sat at one of the small desks, drawing with charcoal on an A3 piece of paper, I kept glancing at the spot where I knew the paint had been the night before, but I could see no evidence of it. Dad did his work well.

Gavin tried to talk to me, but I ignored him.

*

The tough financial times continued. Our visits to the Smith Family for food and clothing became more frequent, and then other charities such as the Salvation Army were added to the rotation. I could sense Dad's impatience building. When I was in bed, I heard him moving around the little house, rarely sitting for long, arranging and rearranging our meagre belongings.

In June, three months after we'd moved into the house in South Sydney, Dad drove us across town to stay at the Glen Mervyn Junior Red Cross Home. The Home was based in an old mansion on Coogee Bay Road in Randwick, a huge red brick building with brown-green moss covering its façade. I remember the trees: gnarled limbs seemingly grabbing for us as we approached, their shadowy knots like glaring eyes. I felt my skin tingle and my fingers shake as I took hold of Dad's hand.

As he led me and my sisters through the large door into the administration building, I could feel tears build in my eyes, but

I fought desperately to hold them back. I didn't want Dad to see me crying, and I knew it wouldn't make him change his mind. The matron was very matter-of-fact about the whole process. Dad handed me my bag, then ruffled my hair.

When I asked how long we'd have to stay, he said, 'I'm not sure Pete. I have some things I need to do.' I hugged his leg until his strong fingers dislodged mine. Then I reluctantly followed the matron up a large winding staircase, to a dormitory on the top floor. It was split through the middle by a large timber wall, boys on one side, girls on the other. There were lots of other kids there. I couldn't see all of them that night, but I could hear them: the shuffling around as they tried to get comfortable on their thin mattresses, their coughs and occasional snoring, a few tears.

At Glen Mervyn, the days were tightly structured. We were woken at 7am sharp and breakfast service would start in the large communal dining room downstairs at 7:15. The food was basic, but I was allowed to eat as much cereal and toast as I wished. As things had been tight at home, I took full advantage of this luxury. All of us were rostered on for duties. We could either clear tables and wash dishes, or clean floors and help with the laundry. I chose tables and dishes, but I would have been happy to work anywhere; it helped to pass the time.

After breakfast, we made our beds and tidied up the metre on either side of our bed and the two metres between the foot of our bed and the foot of the kid opposite. I was surprised to discover that I had been craving this sort of structure and took pride in keeping my little area tidy. After passing the matron's inspection, which I always did on the first go, we were dismissed and had five minutes to get to class.

Our teacher was a young woman named Bethany. She had long blonde hair and always spoke softly. Because I was often first to arrive, she always took time to ask how I was. Despite missing Dad almost constantly, my daily minute speaking with Bethany was a highlight.

After a morning spent learning about Maths and the Humanities from outdated and dogeared textbooks, our afternoons were our own. We were allowed to roam the grounds of the expansive property. I spent most of my spare time with my sisters, particularly Kelly because she was shy and found it so much harder to make friends than Tina and I ever did. We climbed the trees and ran across the open spaces playing endless rounds of tiggy. As I became familiar with my surroundings – and made them my own - I no longer found them frightening.

A couple of times during our stay, we were taken to the beach. This included a stop to the milk bar on the way back to Glen

Mervyn. Then, one day, Dad was waiting for us, leaning against his Holden, arms outstretched. We ran to him. He was in a much better mood than he had been when he dropped us off. On the way home, we stopped at McDonald's, a rare treat, and he told us we could order whatever we wanted. I ordered a Big Mac and a Coke. I also ordered a large serve of French fries, which I dipped into my soft serve to Tina's disgust and Kelly's amusement.

Over the following year, we would return to the Home several times. To this day, I don't know exactly why. All I can do is speculate that Dad knew it was somewhere we would be looked after – somewhere he wouldn't have to worry about us - while he spent his time doing what he did best. At the time, I didn't care why we were there. All I cared about was that he returned. Without fail, I felt an overwhelming relief each time I saw his curly hair and those strong arms open wide.

Now that Dad's financial situation had improved, we spent most of our weekends at the races. The ritual began on Thursday night with Greyhound racing, Friday night was trots, mostly at Harold Park, and Saturday was gallops at either Randwick or Rosehill.

One Saturday, Dad received a hot tip and called a taxi, knowing that it could pull up outside the front gate, allowing him quick access to the betting ring. The taxi pulled up in front our place within 5 minutes.

After exchanging some chit chat with the driver, Dad said, 'If you get us there in twenty minutes, there's an extra 10 bucks in it for you, mate.'

'You got it,' the driver said, before taking off so fast that I was pinned against my black vinyl seat. I glanced past Kelly at Tina, who gave me a wink. She always liked to go fast.

Following Dad's instructions, the driver sped along the backstreets, our tyres squealing as we tore around corners.

Five minutes into the trip, Kelly said, 'Dad, I feel sick.'

Half-turning, Dad said, 'You'll be right, sweetie. We're nearly there.'

The driver had also heard what Kelly said. Perhaps fearing for his upholstery, he flicked on his indicator, but Dad barked, 'Don't stop!' and the driver relented after shooting Dad an annoyed glance.

A few minutes later, the taxi turned into the parking lot. We had just pulled into the drop-off area when Kelly vomited. The vomit dripped down the back of the driver's seat and pooled on the floor as the car filled with an acrid smell that made me want to throw up too.

Immediately, Tina and I slid away from Kelly. 'Gross!' Tina said.

Kelly started to cry. 'I'm so sorry, Dad,' she said through her tears.

The driver pulled off the road, 50 metres short of the designated dropoff point. 'You're not going anywhere until that mess is cleaned up!' He yelled, looking at Dad, then at us.

'Settle down, mate,' Dad said. 'She's just a kid. She can't help it.'

The driver got angrier and started to swear at Dad for not allowing him to pull over and at Kelly for being sick in his car. Dad stopped speaking, then, I saw Tina open her door and take Kelly by the hand. I followed them out of the taxi and I closed the door behind me.

Keeping up a light-hearted stream of conversation, Tina steered us subtlety but deftly away from the taxi. Instinctively, I knew it would be best not to look, but as I heard a car door open and close, I glanced back.

Dad walked around the front of the car, stooped slightly and delivered a single punch to the driver that made him slump onto the steering wheel.

Dad jogged away from the car as its horn blared continuously. I looked up at Dad, then back at the inert figure in the driver's seat, and felt myself go cold inside. Taking my hand, Dad gave me one of his winning smiles, as if nothing was out of the ordinary. Then he said, 'Only 10 minutes to get this bet on, kids. Let's go.'

It was on trips like this one that I developed a range of money-making strategies. Despite our age – I was still only seven at the time – Dad would tell us that he would see us after the last race, then give us a wave and disappear into the crowd. He never gave us money on these trips, so it was up to me to provide for the three of us.

In those days, the patrons - all men - would sit at small tables drinking beer until just before the race began. Then they would leave their seats, and their drinks, to watch the race from the stands. This meant that they would be gone for at least five minutes. While they were gone, I would collect the dregs from the unattended beer glasses, adding them together until I had enough glasses to fill a small cardboard box. Carrying the box to another location, I set it up on a table with a sign leaning up against it. The sign read:

Cold Beer

20c

Cheap

I set my glasses up neatly on a table, now only three-quarters full due to the spillage on my journey, and waited for customers to come. I never had any trouble getting rid of my supply, and always made enough money to buy some treats for me and my sisters, with the balance of the takings going to Dad at the end of the night. The men buying my beer often had a laugh as they threw their coins down on the table, regularly giving me more than the sale price. 'You'll be rich one day,' one said, as he placed a dollar note on the table and took two beers. He walked away chuckling to himself and shaking his head.

My other method of making money didn't attract as much attention as a child selling beer. At the rear of each food van was a large green canvas bag filled with cardboard boxes of ice cream: Peter's Vanilla Hearts. They also contained dry ice which, as well as being fun to play with, kept the stock cold. The Vanilla Hearts were easy pickings. I would take a few boxes, and once-again set up my little shop, this time selling ice-cream at half the price of the food vans. I would only take a box or two from each van, hoping that they wouldn't notice. When they did – which was rare – I knew that there would be no real consequences for a child my age. Dad had taught me that. All I had to remember was not to panic.

The first time I got caught with my stash of discount ice creams, I was marched to the central information booth, where the attendant called Dad's name over the loudspeaker. I waited for him to arrive. When he did, he told the staff how sorry he was and how much trouble I was in. Then he grabbed me firmly by the arm, dragging me behind him until we were out of sight of the booth. There, he gave me a grin and told me to be more careful, then made his way back towards the betting ring.

Once I had exhausted all opportunities for making easy money and my siblings and I had had our fill of junk food, I spent the rest of the night collecting the tote tickets from the ground. Once I had a pile of these, I checked the race results on the screen with the flashing, blurry green text. It was surprising how many people accidentally threw away winning tickets. Sometimes I suspected it was the same people who I had sold beer to earlier in the day, many of whom staggered away from my little stall. As I couldn't collect any of the winnings myself, I waited until the end of the evening until Dad was finished gambling so that he could cash in the tickets.

Dad's mood was directly proportionate to how well he did on the punt. If he had a bad night, we would know about it and the car would be silent on the trip home, all three kids too scared to open our mouths. If he had a win, there were high-fives all round and the mood was jovial. We always hoped that, when Dad returned to us at the end of the races, he did so with a big smile on his face. Sometimes, my collection of tote tickets would pay enough for us to get a take-away. I never felt prouder than watching my family eat and laugh while knowing that I was responsible for making them so happy.

When we weren't at the races, Dad and I would often spend the day at the local TAB while the girls spent the day with friends. Unlike TAB's of today, often located in comfortable Clubs and Pubs, these were smoke-filled shops, with newspapers everywhere and speakers blaring live commentary on races from the major cities, including Sydney, Melbourne and Adelaide, as well as more remote locations such as Dubbo, Scone and Griffith. Despite the din and smell of the TAB, I always enjoyed moments when it was just me and Dad, even if he was distracted, filling out betting slips and listening intently to the results of each race.

As the shop filled up, Dad hurriedly scribbled his selections on the betting slip and moved towards the terminal to place his bet. I walked beside him. I watched as Dad placed his betting slip in front of the operator, a skinny man with long, bony fingers and a moustache stained with nicotine. Without looking up, the operator said, 'Fifty bucks, thanks, mate.'

Dad put his hand to his back pocket to retrieve his wallet, but it wasn't in his the left hand pocket of his jeans. It was *always* in that pocket. He looked back towards the opposite side of the room, where we had been standing, and said, 'Sorry, mate. I must've left it on the bench over there.' The man looked dubiously at my dad as we walked away from his booth.

We crossed the room, and both of us searched through piles of crumpled newspapers, all opened to the sports section, as the race began to run. The wallet was gone. By the time Dad stood up and looked around the room, his face was beet red. I wanted to say something to make him feel better, but I couldn't think of anything. Dad was muttering to himself. Even over the shouts and laughter of the men around us I could hear the words 'It was fucking *here.*'

Finally, Dad reached towards me and I put my hand in his. When his fingers closed around mine, they were too tight. He strode across the room, and I assumed we were leaving. I felt the cool, fresh-smelling air from outside the shop wash over me. Then Dad stopped and turned around, surveying the hundred or more men gathered in the room before letting go of my hand.

In a deft move, Dad grabbed the large vertical handles of both doors, closing them tight and latching them at the bottom and the top. As I watched the short, sharp movements of his shoulders – the way his muscles twitched under his shirt as he moved – my heart began to pound. Suddenly, instinct kicked in and I wrapped my arms around his knee, looking up at him. 'Can't we just leave?' I asked. 'Please?'

Dad didn't answer me. Instead, he used the meaty side of his fist to hammer the door. He kept hitting it until he had the attention of every man in the room. Then he crossed his thick, hairy arms across his large chest and said, 'One of you pricks has my wallet. Nobody is getting through this door until I get it back!'

I was petrified now. The hairs on the back of my neck stood up and I began to shiver despite the heat of the room. I watched the men begin to realise that the doors were locked and my dad wasn't going anywhere.

For a few moments, there was silence. Then somebody cleared his throat and I saw a hand holding a wallet rise above the heads of the crowd. 'Is this yours?' a voice asked.

Instead of answering, Dad strode across the room, as the crowd parted to let him through. He pulled me along behind him. When he was standing in front of the man with the wallet, he fixed him with a look more intense than any I'd ever since in his eyes. 'Where did you find it?' he asked.

The man's face was ashen. He pointed to a spot slightly to his left, where newspapers lay scatted across the floor. I knew for a fact that I had looked through that spot only two minutes before. He was lying. And Dad knew it too.

I waited to see what Dad would do next. Nobody said anything. The only sound was the never-ending racing commentary blaring from the screens above. Then Dad snatched the wallet so deftly that I wasn't sure I'd seen it at all. He flipped it open and counted the cash inside, note by note.

I watched the man watching Dad, and saw the way his hands shook. Suddenly, I felt sorry for him, even though I knew what he had done.

But Dad never touched him. He just looked him over once more, scoffed, and turned on his heel. Then he walked back through the crowd as everybody kept their distance, unlocked the door and steered me outside, his touch gentle but firm.

As we left the TAB behind us, I felt my legs go weak. I knew now what that look in his eyes had meant. If he'd had to, Dad would have fought every one of those men, one by one, until he'd taken back what belonged to him.

# CHAPTER 6

# RUNNING INTO TROUBLE

My 8th birthday came and went with little fanfare. We usually received one present, which was as much as Dad could afford at the time, plus we got to choose where to go for dinner. For me, that was easy: Pizza Hut. This year, Dad had told me I could invite two friends, so I chose Emile and David. Both boys lived in the same court as us.

Emile had been my closest friend for the last year. His mum was French by birth, while his dad was born in Australia. Emile had dark brown curly hair, much like mine, but he was shorter than me, and fatter. Despite our closeness, our parents had never had much to do with each other. Emile had told me, when I slept at his place once, that his parents thought my dad was snobby because he rarely came outside to say hello. I said he just liked to keep to himself. I had actually had to stifle a laugh when I heard the word 'snobby'. It was a word I usually associated with rich people, and whatever else my Dad might be, he had never been rich.

On the day of my birthday, Emile's father walked him over to my house and knocked on the door. I went to greet them while, as usual, my dad stayed inside. I told Emile's Dad that we would be home by 8pm and that I would walk him home. Emile carried a present in his hands, which I pretended not to notice. He gave it to me when we went to the park, where we had decided to play for a couple of hours before we went to Pizza Hut. 'I bet you've been wondering what this is,' he said with a cheeky grin.

I giggled and accepted the gift with both hands. Then I eagerly tore the wrapping paper off. My mouth gaped as I realised what I was holding. 'I saw these on TV!" I said, breathlessly.

Emile smiled as I took the contraption – a Wonderful Waterful Ring Toss - out of its glossy box. The toy was the height of a large book and was designed to be played on a flat surface. Placing it on the patchy grass on the edge of the playground, I pressed a large white button, and the interior, which was filled with water, was shot through with a jet of air, propelling several brightly coloured disks through the liquid. While most of them spun off in different directions and floated to the bottom of the toy's cannister, one did as it was supposed to and fell onto a plastic spike. I cheered. We both laughed.

Over the next hour, Emile and I practiced the ring toss, working out how to press the button with just enough force to land one or more rings on the spikes. Too little force, and they never got close; too much force, and they overshot the spikes, the blast of air sometimes knocking rings that had already been tossed onto the spikes and sending us into cascades of laughter. When we had both had enough of the game, I told Emile that I wanted to play on the equipment. He shrugged and got up, brushing dirt and grass off the front of his jeans and t-shirt. I was halfway to the swing when he called out, 'Bags first swing!'

With my hand already on its chain, I turned around. 'Nah,' I said. 'You go next. Or you can try that one.' I nodded towards the swing next to me, which some bigger kid had obviously yanked too hard, popping the seat off so that it hung off the end of one of the chains.

'I said it was *my turn!*' Emile shouted, serious now, his face reddening right up to his brown curls.

I knew that look. And it made me want to give him the swing even less. It was the look he gave me – and other kids – when he felt he deserved something. As an only child, Emile often felt like he deserved things, and there was nobody at home to tell him no. Today, that would have to be my job. 'No,' I said.

'It's my turn.' He said this in a lower voice, his mouth turning down at the edges. I had never seen that expression on his face before. I wondered whether he was joking, but when I laughed, his eyes just opened wider.

Emile knelt down and felt around in the dirt for a few moments. Then he stood up, holding what I assumed was a clump of mud.

I knew he was angry, but I just didn't want to give in. Still, I said something I probably shouldn't have. Smiling sweetly, I said, 'Why don't you come and give me a push?'

I don't remember seeing the mud leave his hand, but I felt myself fall backwards, off the swing. And I knew straight away that it wasn't mud at all. It was a rock. When I hit the dirt, the air left my lungs with a loud 'Whuuuuh!'

Even as I fought to regain my breath, I could feel a sharp pain above my left eye. I gingerly touched my forehead and my fingers came away hot and wet.

As I forced myself to sit up, blood ran down my face and onto my t-shirt. As I stared down at it, red bloomed on the white fabric, and I was dimly aware that Emile was saying, 'ImsorryImsorryImsorry.' Then he was gone. I watched him run across the park and past my house, towards his own.

Crawling to the other side of the playground, I picked up the Ring Toss and put it securely under my arm. Then I walked home – a journey that felt like it took half an hour although it probably took only a couple of minutes – and stumbled through the front door.

When I entered the lounge, where my dad had been lying down watching the footy, he sprung to his feet. With deft fingers, he held my head back and examined the wound to my scalp. Then he told Kelly to get a wet cloth and he began to clean the wound.

'How bad is it?' I asked.

'Bad enough,' he said, his mouth set. 'Emile did this?'

'Yep.' I nodded, the small motion making my headache worse. 'But he didn't mean it.'

'Not much of a birthday present,' Dad said, simply.

An hour later, I sat on a white padded table while a doctor sewed the wound closed. It took 8 stitches. On our drive home, I asked whether we could still go to Pizza Hut. My dad nodded, and I asked him whether Emile could come, but he shook his head. 'Maybe not such a good idea, kid,' he said.

On the way to the restaurant, we swung past the Court and picked up my other friend, David. He squeezed in between me and Kelly, while Tina sat in the front with Dad. He asked me what happened to my head, and I shrugged. 'Fell off the swing,' I said. I looked up to see Dad glance back at me in the rearview mirror with a look of what I felt was approval.

Pizza Hut was as good as I had remembered. Taking advantage of the restaurant's 'all you can eat' buffet, we all ate pizza and spaghetti Bolognese and garlic bread and jelly and mousse until we felt sick. Even as we ate and laughed, I felt bad for Emile and looked forward to seeing him at school the next week. I wanted to tell him that it didn't matter … that I understood … that we were still friends. But, despite my efforts, we were never as close after that. He didn't come over anymore. After a month or two, I got sick of the Ring Toss and gave it to Kelly, who loved it.

*

For the rest of the year, Dad tried to stay straight. As well as working at our school, he held down a series of short-term cleaning jobs, which he would complete with the three of us in tow. One of these jobs was at a local bank. True to my recent form, I remember going through employees' desks and pocketing loose change and anything else I thought might be of value.

It was during this period that Dad taught me to run. It had begun as something we all did together, but the girls didn't like it and soon gave up, but I kept going, pushing myself, listening to his advice, getting better all the time. I ran in bare feet, and loved the feeling of the grass and dirt passing quickly beneath my toes as I sped across ovals and up and down hills. Whenever I passed him, he would hold up the stopwatch he carried and tell me to keep pushing – that I'd never be successful if I didn't put everything I had into it. His words – his belief, I suppose – made me run faster and longer than I believed I could.

One thing I didn't like about my dad's training regime was breakfast. It consisted of four raw eggs cracked into a glass and stirred, then drunk straight down. I hated the slimy feeling of it sliding down my throat. Another thing was that, even when I wasn't well – and the raw eggs often meant I wasn't – Dad wouldn't let me stop until he decided it was enough. After he saw me vomiting into the bushes on the approach to the finish line one afternoon, he approached me a crooked smile and said, 'You'll thank me for this one day, Pete.'

We had been training for around three months, every afternoon, when Dad showed me the flier. It was for the NSW cross country championships. 'I've entered you in the fifteen hundred metre race. Most of the kids will be a year older than you, so it'll be a good test.'

Instantly, my stomach did cartwheels and I felt nauseous. I had so many questions. I had never raced anyone except my dad and my siblings before, and fifteen hundred metres sounded like a long way. Dad explained that it would mean running for three-hundred metres, then three times around the oval. I was too nervous, and excited, to say anything.

The race meet was scheduled for the following weekend. I could think of little else as the big day approached. That morning, Dad got me up early and told me to skull some raw eggs. Then he peeled a banana and smothered it in peanut butter before instructing me to eat it. The thought of all those ingredients mixing together in my stomach only added to my queasiness, but I forced them down and sat at the kitchen, staring at the clock on the wall. Two hours until race time.

At nine-thirty, we hopped in the car and headed off on a short journey to the track. None of us spoke. We arrived in plenty of time, but everybody else seemed to have gotten there before us. There were tall boys stretching and running in short bursts, warming up. I couldn't believe that I would have to face them in just a few minutes.

Dad took me to the registration table and they handed me a plastic bib with the number 3 on it. 'Maybe that's a good omen,' the kind-faced woman at the registration table said, patting the number. 'You might get a place.' There was something about her voice that made me feel uncomfortable. Something *churchy*. I forced a smile.

Dad attached the bib to my singlet. The fabric was white when we'd begun training months ago; now, it was a pale yellow with dark rings around the neck and under both arms. Dad was speaking, I realised. I tried to tune in, to understand what he was saying, but I couldn't make sense of it. Something about the race. And strategy. Keep to the inside line. Let someone else take the lead. Sit in third or fourth. Let them set the pace.

Finally, I found myself on the staggered starting line, in the middle of a pack of at least fifteen kids. I noticed two boys staring at my bare feet. One of them laughed. Then the other one laughed too.

I glanced around me, and realised that I was the only one who wasn't wearing shoes. I could see the other boys' running spikes gleaming where they met the ground. I knew that I could run perfectly well without shoes, but my face still burned as I heard the boys' laughter. All I wanted now was to beat them both.

'Alright, boys', said a man with a pot belly and a starter pistol. 'On your marks.' He scanned our feet to ensure they weren't in front of the line. 'Set.'

I leaned forward, staring at the tan-coloured track in front of me.

Bang!

The pistol shot rang in my ears. Then I heard a cheer rise from the spectators in the stadium. We were off.

I tried to settle into a comfortable spot, third or fourth from the leading runner, but I was knocked around by the bigger boys around me as they jostled for position. Soon after, we began our first lap of the oval. As I began to feel more comfortable with the pace, I tried to run around a boy with bright white sneakers, but somebody ran between us, sending me into the second lane and almost causing me to trip. I stumbled, then found my rhythm again, but was shocked to discover that I was behind all but one of the competitors.

By the time we completed our first lap, my chest had begun to ache. I started to panic, knowing that I could never match the frantic pace set by the race leader. Then I felt the pack slow a little and my breath began to calm. I told myself not to think so much about the other boys and looked down at my own feet pounding the track. A couple of times, I risked a glance at the stands, but couldn't see my dad or my sisters. Instead, I watched the boys' coaches on the sidelines, shouting instructions or waving their hands, making signals I didn't understand.

When we began our second lap, I was still at the rear of the pack. If I was going to try to catch up, it would have to be soon. I pumped my arms and felt my pace increase slightly, allowing me to get my shoulders ahead of one boy, then another. Ahead of me, I could see the pack leader. It was the boy who had laughed at my bare feet.

As we began our final lap, a tall, thin man on the sidelines rang a bell. The crowd cheered louder. My legs and lungs burned as the boys at the front of the pack accelerated with less than 300 meters to go. I wanted to try to catch them, but my dad's instructions rang in my ears: 'Don't go too early, son. Wait for the back straight, about 200 meters out. Then give it everything you have left.' I ran on, focusing on my breathing, but watching for the sign.

Then I saw the marker indicating that we had reached the back straight. This was it.

Forgetting the pain, I pushed my legs harder than I'd ever pushed them in training.

I was fourth now.

I sped up, and the boy next to me gave up and fell away.

Third.

We rounded the final bend. The boy in front of me was a few metres ahead and running strongly. It was the kid who had laughed at me. His legs looked powerful, but his shoulders had begun to slump. He was tired. I sped up. Drew alongside him. He made the mistake of turning his head ... and I passed him.

Second.

From the corner of my right eye, I thought I saw Dad in the stands. He was on his feet now. I felt my heart lift. The pain disappeared. I was breathing clearly, every breath filling my muscles with energy. I was unstoppable.

I pulled to my right and tried to draw up next to the leader. He sensed me at his shoulder and stepped in front of me, blocking my path.

For a moment, I lost momentum. I looked past the leader and saw the finish line just ahead. Then, without giving myself a chance to second-guess my decision, I went wide – *too wide*, almost – but I swerved at the last moment, stretching my legs straight out and pulling slightly ahead. The leader kicked his legs out further, matching my stride.

As the finish line beckoned, we both lunged, chests out.

I had no idea who won until I saw Dad, Tina and Kelly running towards me. The girls were jumping up and down with excitement, and Dad's eyes were gleaming. 'You did it, son!' Dad yelled, hugging me to him. 'You bloody did it!'

After the medal presentation, one of the officials approached Dad and they stood together for a couple of minutes, speaking quietly. She glanced at me a couple of times as they spoke, her blue eyes filled with compassion. When they were finished, Dad thanked her and approached us kids. We walked back to the car in silence.

We were almost home when I asked Dad what the woman had wanted to talk to him about. His face reddened, and I wondered whether I'd said the wrong thing.

Dad took a deep breath. 'She said her club would like to buy you some running shoes, Pete. Shoes with spikes.'

I felt a rush of excitement as I imagined lacing up a pair of new runners like the ones the other boys wore. Then I saw the look in Dad's eyes and knew what his answer had been. 'You told her no,' I said.

Dad shook his head. 'I told her you didn't need 'em. Before you started to run, none of those people – that nice lady included – none of them believed in you, did they?' I shook my head, and he squeezed my shoulder softly. 'Well, they do now.'

We were in the middle of dinner, and Kelly was recounting the story of the race for the third time, when Dad put a finger to his lips, indicating that she should stop speaking. She did so and Dad said, 'I know you're not gonna like this, kids, but today was our last day in this place.'

'In this house?' Tina asked, hopefully, but we all knew the answer. This city.

'Only grab what you need,' Dad said.

Half an hour later, as I packed my bag, I listened to both girls crying in their bedroom. It felt crueler, somehow, after the high of the afternoon's win. Then Dad was steering us into the car, loading our suitcases into the boot, and we were pulling away from our house, our school, and our friends.

'Bye, house,' Kelly said.

'Bye, house,' Tina said.

I said nothing. I knew better than to ask why we were leaving or where we would end up. As long as we stayed together, I could handle anything.

# CHAPTER 7

# A FRAGILE HOPE

It was bitterly cold when Dad opened the door and the breeze hit my face, shocking me awake. We had stopped to grab fuel, seemingly in the middle of nowhere. I turned around to see both girls asleep across the back seat, Tina letting out a little snore every few seconds.

After Dad had paid for the fuel, he climbed back into the car. 'Where are we headed?' I asked, my voice croaky with sleep.

'Bendigo,' Dad said. He sounded tired. 'We'll have to stay in emergency housing until I find something more permanent.' His head hung for a moment, and I felt my heart swell with pain for him. 'I know it's not ... ideal, but it's our only option right now.'

It was still dark when we pulled up at a large, single-story building in one of the back streets of Bendigo and Dad got out. He had placed his woollen jumper over me at some point during out trip and I pulled it tighter around me as I watched him approach a white brick façade that seemed to glow in the moonlight. Dad pressed the little black bell fixed to the wall next to the main set of doors and waited.

Behind me, the girls had begun to stir.

Somebody buzzed Dad in. He was gone for a few minutes, then walked back to the car and started the engine without saying a word. He steered the car quietly down a long driveway, then pulled to a stop in the dark shadow of a large tree and told us to grab our stuff.

A minute later, we entered a small cabin with hessian curtains and a low-wattage bulb in the ceiling. Under its feeble light, I saw a tiny kitchen stove and a small round table with four rickety chairs. There was only one bedroom, which had two sets of bunks. The girls took one, and I climbed onto the top bunk of the other. The pillow was a little scratchy under my cheek, so I lay my head on Tom the Turtle instead.

Dad checked on me, tucking me in tightly and ruffling my hair. Then he tucked the girls in and climbed into the bunk below mine. I was staring at the moon through the hessian curtain when I was overtaken by sleep once more.

Although we didn't have a home of our own, we were enrolled at the local primary school. Dad wasn't working, so our routine became simple: walking to and from school, eating something in our tiny kitchen, reading books from the school library, and sleeping.

I looked forward to our weekly trip to the milk bar a couple of kilometres away, which we reached by walking along the gumtree-lined street beside the railway track, my hand in dad's. While we walked, he told us stories of what it had been like for him growing up. I knew, instinctively, that *our* childhood had been pretty tough, but his sounded worse. Even so, he told the stories with a fondness that made even the toughest events seem like adventures.

When we reached the milk bar, we were greeted by the sweet, fruity smell of lollies. Dad gave us each 20 cents to spend and bought himself a newspaper. The shopkeeper, an Indian man who wore a turban and had a nicotine-stained moustache, filled up a small white paper bag with lollies shaped like bananas, raspberries, milk bottles, and – my favourite – a little set of false teeth. On our way home, I would wear these candy teeth over my real teeth while Kelly squealed with laughter. I could make a bag of lollies last the rest of the day, sucking each one until it became a sweet translucent wafer.

While Kelly and I were able to grudgingly accept the mundanity of our routine, Tina was becoming restless and disobedient – even rude. She had just started high school and was hanging out with the cool group. Most of her attention seemed to be focused on one boy in particular: Brett. He was one of the popular boys at school and would often ride his dirt bike to our house despite being unlicensed. He was several years older than Tina and she clearly wanted to impress him, often coming home late despite Dad's admonitions.

Dad was always civil to Brett, which surprised me slightly. Even *I* knew there was something off about him. I hated the way he would listen to Dad, nodding and saying, 'Yes, yep, I understand,' and then start smirking as soon as Dad turned his back. I would watch these exchanges from my secret 'base' in the rec centre, twenty or thirty metres away from our cabin.

We had been staying in our cabin for two or three weeks when a delivery of Bradford Bats arrived. Whoever had delivered them had left around one-hundred bats stacked neatly on the rec centre's veranda. Dad said they would eventually be used to insulate each of the property's cabins, to keep families warmer in winter and cooler in summer, but that we'd most likely have moved out by then.

One morning, when the others were still asleep, I walked over to the rec centre and – leaving some of the pink bats in the front where they were, I began turning those behind them on their sides and making them stand upright, forming a small tunnel that I could close by propping another bat up against the opening from inside. Inside my base, I continued my excavations, twisting and turning the bats until I had formed an entire room. I then shifted a few of the outside bats just enough to give myself a bit of light. In my base, I felt warm and safe.

I spent hours in there, sucking on lollies I'd stored away and reading a couple of crumpled comics that one of my new school friends had given me. I considered telling my sisters about my hiding place but decided against it. Tina was getting too old and would probably make fun of me, and Kelly was likely to tell Dad, who might tell me to stop playing there.

Another game I used to play in my base was cops and robbers. I was the robber, hanging out in my secret fortress. Anybody who walked past the rec centre was a cop. I would watch them walk by, feeling a sense of triumph when they had left and I remained undetected.

This was how I saw Tina and Brett arrive home on his dirt bike the first time he came over, and how I saw Dad talk to him afterwards.

I was in my base one evening, re-reading a *Fantastic Four* comic, when Dad called for me. I crawled outside, replaced the door, and trotted over to our cabin. Even before I arrived, I smelled sausages. My stomach rumbling, I sat at the dining table while Dad served me white bread with two snags and sauce. I had picked up my sausages in bread and was about to take a bite when I realised that neither of the girls was eating. Kelly's eyes were lowered, while Tina's face was red and blotchy, her eyes puffy. When she caught me looking at her, she said, 'What?'

I just shrugged and started to eat.

Later, when we were brushing our teeth, Kelly whispered that Dad had told Tina she wasn't allowed to hang out with Brett anymore. I wondered why he'd finally made the decision, but secretly felt happy about it. After saying goodnight to Dad and my sisters, I climbed into my bunk and fell asleep quickly.

Sometime later, I woke with a start. At first, I didn't know what had roused me, until I heard it again: a knock on the door. Then I heard Dad's voice, saying, 'Alright, coming.' A moment later, I heard the door creak open and another man's voice say, 'Mister Halliwell?' Halliwell was the name we'd been using since we had arrived at the cabin.

Suddenly, I had a bad feeling. I climbed down the wooden ladder from my bunk and dropped silently to the floor, a move I'd practiced a hundred times. Then I walked out into the little hallway and into the kitchen, where Dad was standing at the door, facing two men in suits. I didn't need anybody to tell me they were cops.

Sidling up to my father, I put my hand in his. His skin felt warm but sweatier than usual.

I looked up at the men. They looked down at me. The cops I imagined when I played in my base were hard-faced and threatening. Neither of these men seemed like that.

Both wore name badges. Officer Collins had a dark moustache that ran the length of his upper lip, and a hard face that looked like he had seen his fair share of trauma and sadness. There was something in his expression that reminded me of my dad's. Officer Reynolds was younger, with a buzz cut and no facial hair. He gave me a little smile. I didn't smile back.

Officer Collins was the first to speak. Looking at Dad, he cleared his throat and said, 'Do you have a daughter named Tina?'

'Yes,' Dad replied.

'And is she … um … at home, sir?'

I had never imagined a policeman calling my father 'sir'.

'It's almost midnight,' Dad said, a little sharply. 'Of course she's home. She was in bed around 8.'

'Could I … ah … trouble you to check, sir?' Officer Collins said, chewing his lip.

Dad let go of my hand as he made the short trip from the front door to our bedroom. As we walked past the single armchair, I noticed a couple of beer bottles on the floor and knew that Dad must have fallen asleep while sitting in his chair again.

Dad quietly pushed our bedroom door open, and I saw his shoulders relax as he was confronted with a lump under the covers on the bottom bunk.

On the bunk above, Kelly sat up. She was lit by the light streaming through the open door. 'What's happening, Dad?' she asked. Dad stepped closer to her and patted her hair reassuringly, then helped her to lie down.

After Kelly had resettled, Dad leaned over. He was reaching for Tina when his hand froze. With a rough motion, he pulled the bedclothes off the lump beneath, revealing three pillows, arranged to look like someone was in the bed. When he turned around, his face was flushed and he was breathing hard.

'She's not here,' Dad said. 'What the hell is going on?'

Again, Officer Collins cleared his throat, then looked straight at Dad. 'I'm sorry to tell you this, Mister Halliwell. Your daughter, Tina, has been involved in a serious accident.'

I watched Dad slump against the bed. Stepping forward, the younger officer reached out instinctively, but Dad pulled away from the hand he offered.

'What ...?' Dad began, then said, 'How ...?'

'She was riding a motorbike,' Officer Reynolds said. 'You need to make your way to Bendigo Hospital immediately.' He glanced at the couple of bottles of beer sitting beside the lounge chair. 'If you think you're okay to drive.'

'Of course I am,' Dad said, angrily. Then his voice softened as he said, 'Is she … going to be … okay?'

Officer Reynolds looked like he was about to answer, but then turned to his senior officer, who responded instead. 'We don't have accurate information right now, Mister Halliwell. It's better that you go to speak directly with her doctors.'

Neither Kelly nor I needed to be told to get in the car. A minute later, we were buckling ourselves into the back seat, while Dad climbed into the front. As he turned the key in the ignition, I thought I saw a tear on his cheek, but he wiped it away with a slash from his shirtsleeve and threw the car in gear.

Kelly and I held hands all the way to the hospital. As the double-glass doors opened and the bright white lights of the emergency department stung my eyes, my stomach began to churn.

Dad strode to the front desk and asked which room Tina was in. The nurse was young and pretty, with red hair tied up in a bun. She told Dad to take a seat and assured him that a doctor would be with us shortly. Within a couple of minutes, a young man in a white coat appeared and said, 'Mister Halliwell?'

Nodding, Dad stood, and followed the doctor to the edge of the waiting room, where neither Kelly nor I could hear what they were saying. I watched Dad's body language carefully. For a minute, he just nodded, his back and shoulder muscles tense. Then he seemed to slump slowly, as if all the breath had left him. I watched the Doctor's face tighten with worry. Then Dad stood up straight again, turned on his heel and walked back over to us. When he took our hands, his face was drawn and pale.

In silence, the three of us followed the doctor down a series of white-lit hallways, their walls and floors lined in the same off-white plastic. I quickly lost any sense of where the outside world was. Then we reached another pair of glass doors, these ones adorned with red letters: INTENSIVE CARE. I wasn't sure what the words meant, but I knew instinctively that they weren't good.

Inside the intensive care unit, there was no chit-chat between the nursing staff. They moved busily from room to room, where people lay under sheets, some with arms or legs suspended from pulleys and covered with bandages or casts, all attached to little monitors beside their beds, with wires carrying fluid in and out of their bodies. As we approached a room on the opposite side of the unit, I wanted to run away. Then I saw how bravely Kelly was behaving and knew that I had to be strong too. For Tina. And for Dad.

When we entered the room at the end of the hall, I froze. There were more tubes and wires attached to the girl in the bed than I thought was possible. The machine beside her beeped on and off, while a green wave showed fluctuations in her heart rate. One leg and one arm were already in plaster and her head had been wrapped in a white bandage, leaving only one of her eyes and a thin slice of her face visible. The skin that I could see was purple and swollen, while the skin around the eye was black, making it almost impossible to recognise her. But I knew it was Tina.

Suddenly, Kelly burst into tears and ran from the room. Dad followed her, leaving me standing beside Tina's bed with only the doctor for company. He pulled a chair out from against the wall and steered me into it. I sat back against the hard cushion and stared at Tina. When the doctor left, I wondered whether I should leave too. Then, without thinking about it, I leaned forward and held Tina's hand, making sure not to disturb the tubes sticking out of it. I gave her fingers a squeeze, hoping to see her swollen eye flutter open, but she remained still.

When somebody else entered the room, I assumed it was my dad, but I looked up to see a man in a black robe. I recognised him as a priest from the times my foster family had taken me to church for Christmas, Easter, and weddings. His expression was serious. 'Is your father here?' he asked. I was about to answer when Dad entered the room, holding Kelly in his arms. Her face was pressed against his neck.

Turning to Dad, the priest said, 'I am here to offer … comfort, if you like. To Tina.'

Dad nodded. He was crying openly now.

For a couple of minutes, the priest spoke in a soft voice. Then he dabbed holy water on Tina's exposed forehead, touched my Dad's shoulder, and left.

The ritual over, Dad wiped his eyes and looked at me. He gave me a tiny smile and I smiled back.

That night, we slept in Tina's hospital room. Kelly and I shared a bed at the foot of Tina's bed. Dad had said he would sleep in the chair, but whenever I opened my eyes – usually on the hour, when a nurse came to check on Tina – I saw he was still awake.

The next morning, the same doctor who had showed us into Tina's room appeared and checked her over. He appeared mildly surprised and told Dad that her vital signs had 'picked up'. When Dad asked what that meant, the doctor said, 'It means you shouldn't give up hope.'

We left the hospital around 10am and drove half an hour back to our cabin, where we showered, ate and slept for a few hours. Then Dad drove us back to the hospital so we could keep up our vigil. This became our routine for the next two weeks, as Tina remained in intensive care, unconscious. A few times, the doctor told Dad that it might be 'time', which meant that we wouldn't go back to the cabin. Then he would appear and say that Tina had improved slightly, and we would be allowed to leave once more.

It was a cold Tuesday morning when Tina finally woke up.

Over the last couple of weeks, the sliver of her face that was visible between bandages had become more recognisable as the bruising and swelling began to subside. Now, the eye, eyebrow and cheek were recognisably hers. I was sitting next to her, holding her hand as usual. Bored, I tickled her arm, and felt her fingers jump beneath mine. Then her eyelid opened a crack. 'Pete?' she whispered, her voice faint and confused.

'Dad!' I cried out. 'She's awake!'

Suddenly Dad and Kelly were by my side, leaning over the bed, hugging her, then apologising as she groaned.

'Dad?' Tina said. 'Where am I?'

I stood up and Dad sat down, holding Tina's hand gently and speaking softly. 'You've had an accident,' he said. He pressed the red button beside the bed and, moments later, a nurse entered. When she saw that Tina was awake, she ran from the room. She returned in less than a minute, the doctor in tow. 'Well,' he said, as he approached Tina's bed, 'You *are* a tough one.'

Tina didn't answer. She continued looking around the room, seemingly still trying to figure what she was doing there.

Only later did I learn how close she came to death. Apparently, the doctor told Dad the fact that Tina didn't end up with brain damage was as close to a miracle as he had seen.

As Tina continued to improve and we prepared for her to come home, Dad turned his attention to learning what had happened the night of the accident. The doctor provided him with a copy of the accident report, and I found him sitting at our kitchen table one morning, reading with his fists clenched. I knew instinctively not to approach him, but when he finished reading, I asked what was wrong.

'He never even came to visit,' Dad said, his eyes on the report. 'The little bastard!' Dad pounded the table once, sharply, tipping over the pepper grinder and making me jump. 'Doing a hundred k on a windy road. At night. Of course *he* was wearing a helmet.'

Dad remained focused on Tina's recovery. When she finally returned to the cabin, he did his best to make sure that she was comfortable on her bunk, and would help her to the toilet several times a day, waiting outside until she was done and then half-walking her, half-carrying her back to bed. Only once did I hear him ask her about Brett – what his last name was, where he lived – but Tina wouldn't tell him, so he dropped it.

I suspect that, under other circumstances, Dad would have found some other way of locating Brett. As it was, we had received several follow-up visits from Officers Collins and Reynolds. Late one afternoon, I heard them talking to Dad about an upcoming court appearance and charges, including negligent driving. After they left, Dad appeared nervous. I knew instinctively that it was the mention of court.

Because of this, I wasn't surprised when he announced that it was time for us to leave Bendigo. Tina was still fragile, but he said she could recover anywhere.

It was the middle of the day when we left the cabin. I didn't even bother asking where we were going. I simply buckled myself into the back seat, while Tina tried to find a comfortable position in the front.

As we drove, the trees outside my window seemed to blur together. I wondered whether this was how we would always live: dodging the cops, using fake names. Would we ever stay long enough anywhere for it to feel like home?

# Chapter 8

# WHEN THE WALLS CAME DOWN

After running for so long, the end – when it came – was at least quick.

Our latest accommodation was a Salvation Army Emergency Housing facility outside Shepparton. Much like the last place we'd stayed, we were given a unit that sat a little way off the main road; however, this time, the cabin had two bedrooms. The girls shared one, while Dad and I shared the other.

Another difference between this and the last place was the on-site 'shop'. Located in a back room in the main office building, it was open to all residents. We had been allowed to visit the shop the day we arrived, where we found shelf-lined walls, each crammed full of clothing. The facility's manager, a short, round guy with a thick white beard, told us we could take a couple of things each, which only added to the impression that he was like Santa Claus.

After arriving in Shepparton, we spent most of our time inside our cabin. Sometimes, we ventured out, to kick a ball back and forth in the dusty space between cabins; this passed for our garden. I asked Dad when we could go to school, and he said he wasn't sure yet … that he was 'working things out'. I assumed, because of this, that we were only passing through Shepparton, but three weeks after we arrived, we were still there. One reason for Dad's willingness to stop for so long in the otherwise unremarkable facility was Rosie.

Dad had met Rosie a couple of days after we arrived. She was running from an abusive husband – I'd heard her telling Dad about him late at night as they sat at the little table in our kitchen. I heard other things, too: noises I didn't recognise, that made me feel squirmy inside and made it hard to look at Dad after Rosie left and he returned to the room we shared. Lying there one night, in the dark, he said, 'How would you feel if I invited Rosie to travel with us for a while?'

I shrugged. 'Okay, I guess.' And, that night, I felt like it really would be okay. So long as I still had Dad, I didn't care about anything else. I knew my sisters would feel the same way.

On my tenth birthday, I woke to the smell of pancakes. In the kitchen, Kelly and Tina were sitting at the table while Dad cooked. 'Happy birthday, kiddo,' he said, picking me up and kissing me on the cheek — a rarity. Then he said, 'Look what we got ya.'

The girls were each holding a present. I unwrapped them to find the *Guinness Book of Records* from Kelly and a Matchbox car from Tina. I knew we didn't have any money – we were only having pancakes because Santa Claus had brought us some vouchers for the local Woolworths – so I told Dad I didn't need these things. But he said, 'Hey, hey, none of that. You deserve it.'

I was playing with the Matchbox car, a red, black and silver Corvette, making it perform skids and jumps in the recreation area, when I heard a man shouting in one of the other cabins. I couldn't place where the voice was coming from, but I felt like I knew who the speaker was.

We were staying in Unit 4. Rosie was in Unit 3. In Unit 2 was an old, wiry man who sat on a low stool on his front stoop, chain-smoking menthol cigarettes in silence. That only left Unit 1, which was occupied by a husband and wife. She was small, with curly red hair. He was tall and fat, his arms, legs and belly covered with tattoos only half-visible beneath tangled body hair.

The man continued to shout – at his wife, I imagined – for at least a minute. Then Rosie emerged from her unit, a grimace on her face. Moments later, my dad opened the front door. I watched him look at Rosie, then at Unit 1, before he closed the flywire door and leaned back against the doorframe. Kelly or Tina must have tried to open the door, because I saw him half-turn his head and heard him say, 'Stay inside.' His tone was hard.

The abuse went on for another couple of minutes, while all of us remained where we were as if frozen. Then, from inside Unit 1, I heard something shatter. It must have been crockery, or a glass, because even at this distance, the high, sharp note continued to ring in my ears as I watched Dad cross the common area and stop outside Unit 1.

From my vantage point, the flywire screen made everything inside the cabin appear indistinct. I watched what appeared to be a large shadow fill the doorframe and heard a deep male voice say, 'What the fuck do you want?'

When Dad spoke, it was in a softer tone that he'd used with my sister moments ago. It was the kind of tone he used when he wanted to calm things down. 'Just wanted to ask whether you're almost done.'

The door of Unit 1 opened and the man stepped out, folding his inked arms over his massive chest. 'What's it to you?'

'I've got a couple of kids here,' Dad said, nodding in our general direction. 'They don't like hearing the shouting. That's all.'

For a moment, the guy nodded, as if considering my dad's words. Then he pointed to me and said, 'You can tell your kids to go fuck themselves.'

For a moment, Dad said nothing, but I saw his shoulders and back tense. My stomach clutched and I feared what he would do. Then he took a deep breath and stepped away from the man in the doorway. 'Alright. Have a good day,' he said.

I saw how red his face was. The way he couldn't meet my eyes. I knew what he wanted to do. And I knew why he couldn't do it.

Dad was halfway across the recreation area, approaching our unit, when the man stepped off his front porch. Now, I could make out the shape of his wife through the flywire door. She was sitting on the edge of the sofa, shaking with sobs. Seeing her made me think of my own mum, of the woman I imagined her to be, and I felt like I might cry, suddenly.

I glanced at the man just as one side of his mouth curled upwards. 'Who are you, anyway …?' he asked, 'To come here judging me, telling me how to act?' The guy was smiling now. 'You're a fucking embarrassment to your kids, mate.'

Dad stopped walking. He shook his head.

I wanted to stand up, to tell Dad not to listen, but I couldn't make my mouth work.

I watched Dad turn back to the man and take a deep breath. Then I heard him say, 'And you're a fat, tattooed pig.'

The man wasn't smiling anymore. One moment, his face flushed red; the next, he launched himself at Dad, tacking him around the chest and driving him into the dirt.

Dad couldn't get out from under him, so he did the next best thing: he hit the guy with his elbow, aiming for his eye. As soon as his elbow made contact, blood sprang from the cut, and he aimed at the same place again, hitting him twice more.

When the man pulled away slightly, Dad got out from under him and followed up the elbows with an attempted knee to the chin, but the man was surprisingly quick despite his size and managed to block it. He punched Dad twice, in the ribs, then the face, before Dad punched him back. Again, the guy launched himself at Dad. Again, they hit the ground.

Now, there was no doubt Dad was losing. His attacker was just too big. As Dad clawed at his forearms, the fat man climbed astride his chest and wrapped one hand around Dad's throat, then the other. He began to squeeze, with all his strength, the veins standing out on his own neck with the effort.

Dad could only splutter as he choked, his face growing red, then purple.

Somebody was screaming. Maybe it was me.

Then I saw somebody else within the cloud of dust that surrounded the two warring men. It was the old, wiry man. He was holding something above his head. It was his favourite wooden stool.

With surprising speed, the old man brought the stool down over the back of the fat man's skull. It made a cracking sound, and the stool snapped in half. The fat man dropped immediately, his face plowing into the dirt just beside Dad's head. For a few moments, Dad was stuck underneath him, before the old man and Rosie managed to roll him off.

The fat man was out cold. Blood from the cut above his left eye, and from the back of his head, began to pool around his skull.

'Fucking bully,' the old man said, spitting at the fat man's prone form. Then he held out his hand and helped Dad up.

We returned to our unit, where Rosie put on the kettle and made Dad a cup of tea. He was halfway through drinking it when I heard the same angry voice I'd heard earlier yelling, 'Hey! What the fuck? HEY!' When nobody answered, he yelled, 'Once I get this head fixed up, I'll be back. Then I'm going to murder your entire family.'

Kelly began to cry. Dad sipped his tea and put his arm around her. 'It'll be alright,' he said. 'You'll see. He's all talk. They always are.' But, as nighttime fell and the fat man returned to the facility, I saw Dad lock the front door and place a rolling pin on the kitchen counter. He'd asked Rosie whether she wanted to stay for a while after dinner, and they were still watching the small, black and white TV when I went to bed.

Under my covers that night, I kept expecting to hear the fat man's steps outside our door and his fist pound the wood. Or maybe – I imagined – he'd tear the door off its hinges like one of the bad guys in my comics: a real-life Juggernaut. I was surprised when I heard a banging on the front door and realised that I'd been asleep for some time. It was now completely dark inside the unit, and Dad was snoring softly beside me.

Terrified as I remembered the fat man's vow, I shook Dad's shoulder. He woke with a start, and started to ask, 'What is…?' but there was another pounding on the front door and he was suddenly upright.

'Shit!' Dad said.

A moment later, he was at the bedroom door, his shoulder and curly hair highlighted by the moonlight spilling through the front curtains.

'Dad?' I asked. 'What does he want?'

Dad turned back to me. He looked like he was about to say something reassuring when there was a crash and the sound of wood splintering. Then multiple voices screamed, 'Down! Down! Down!' and the living room was filled with men. Somebody threw Dad against the bedroom's doorframe, before slapping handcuffs on his wrists and snapping them shut.

At first, I was too shocked to cry. But when I walked into the hallway and saw the girls at their bedroom door with tears running down their cheeks, my own tears came. I cried harder when Dad asked whether he could have a moment to cuddle us. He knelt down and we hugged him, one at a time. Kelly went first; then Tina. When it was my turn, he said, 'Look after your sisters, Petey.'

I nodded.

'I love you,' Dad said.

I wanted to tell him that I loved him too, but as soon as I opened my mouth to speak, I started to sob.

The men pulled Dad to his feet and marched him towards the front door.

We followed him outside, and I was about to run up to him when I felt a hand on my shoulder and turned to see Rosie looking down at me with a pitying smile. 'It'll be okay,' she said. 'I'm sure it's just a mix-up.'

As the cops drove Dad away, Kelly, Tina and I huddled together in the dust and the dark. The adults moved around us, talking, making comforting noises, asking whether we wanted something to eat or drink, telling us to come inside. But we just held each other. Already, I knew things would never be the same.

# Chapter 9

# IN THE HANDS OF STRANGERS

The next day, Kelly and I were transported to Shepparton Police Station and left to sit alone in a room that had nothing more than a bare table and 4 chairs. The walls were clean and white and I could smell they had been freshly painted. Different people came and went. There were lots of conversations happening outside the room, but I couldn't make out the words.

My sister and I didn't speak. What was the point? Neither of us knew what would happen next. Neither of us were in control.

Finally, a middle-aged woman entered the room and introduced herself as a caseworker from Child Welfare Authority Victoria. She had short auburn hair and thick-rimmed glasses. She spoke softly and seemed genuinely sorry for us. She told us her name was Angela. I thought it sounded like 'angel'. But I already knew there was no such thing, and tried to put the thought out of my mind.

Angela told us that Dad would probably be spending a significant time in jail and it was her job was to find us some immediate care.

She asked us some questions and noted down our answers. As she wrote, I noticed her fingers shake, and I started to feel nervous. Then she put down her pen and spoke to us at length.

Angela said that Kelly and I would be made state wards. I sneaked a peek at Kelly and saw that she was as confused as I was. Speaking slowly and carefully, Angela explained that the State of Victoria would become our legal guardians. From now on, the government would make all decisions regarding our welfare, including where we would go to school, who we would live with, when we would go to the doctors, and when clothes would be supplied to us.

I remember the feeling of dread in my stomach as she spoke. I couldn't understand how this woman – or the government she represented – expected to be able to replace my Dad. He would come back one day, wouldn't he? I knew that, if he was here, Dad would fix everything somehow. But he wasn't here. That was the point.

By the time she left, Angela looked pale and exhausted. Kelly and I were left in the small white room, sitting opposite one another, for what felt like hours. Finally, I heard people speaking outside the door. I still couldn't make out the words, but their conversation sounded urgent.

When I met Kelly's gaze, I knew what she was thinking. She was tired. She wanted to go home. But where was home, exactly?

Eventually, Angela returned. She lowered herself into one of the seats and opened her mouth to speak, but nothing came out. Then she took a deep breath and said, 'The good news is that we've found a family for your sister Tina to stay with. A nice family. We think she'll be very happy there.'

This didn't feel like good news. I wanted to ask when we could see Tina, but Angela went on: 'Unfortunately, we haven't been able to secure suitable foster care for the two of you. Not yet, anyway. Which means you won't be able to stay together. Instead —"

For a moment, she looked at her feet. Then she looked up again, her eyes filled with tears. I watched one tear, then another, trickle down the soft, white skin of her cheek as she explained, 'You're going to be taken to Melbourne, where you'll spend some time in a youth detention centre. Separate centres, actually. One for boys, the other for girls.'

'What's a detention centre?' I asked.

'It means jail,' Kelly said, her tone flat. 'Kids' jail.'

Now, Angela was crying openly. She told us that she wished she could take us both home with her. I felt terrible: for us, and for her.

Already, I had learned that sometimes good people have to make tough decisions. After a few moments, I crossed the room, put my arms around Angela, and felt her body shudder against mine. 'We'll be okay,' I said softly. 'Really. Dad will come and find us soon. You'll see.' This only made her cry more.

Finally, Angela walked me and Kelly to a police car and waved goodbye as we drove away. We rode in silence to Shepparton Airport, where a small plane was waiting.

We had never been on a plane before, but, given the circumstances, neither of us were excited. All I remember about the flight was that the plane – an 8-seater – was small and noisy. The whole flight, I stared out the window and thought about Tina and Dad. I hoped they were both okay, wherever they were.

We landed in Melbourne and walked out of the terminal to where two unmarked cars waited. I hugged Kelly and she hugged me back tightly. Neither of us said anything. Then a police officer opened the rear door of one of the cars and I climbed inside.

As we drove away from the airport, I looked around the inside of the vehicle, thinking about the times my Dad had been taken away in cars much like this one. I wondered whether he felt the same fear that I felt now.

After what felt like a long time, we slowed down and turned onto a driveway that extended towards a double-storey building in the distance. The driveway was flanked by high brick fences, and I saw the name of the place illuminated by the car's headlights: BALTARA RECEPTION CENTRE.

The officers took me to an administration building, where one of them signed a piece of paper. After giving me a curt nod, he left me sitting in a waiting room, on an uncomfortable green plastic chair. A few minutes later, a man entered the room. He wore white pants and a green shirt the same colour as the plastic waiting room chairs. He was tall and otherwise thin but with a round potbelly that protruded over his belt. 'Peter?' he asked, his thin lips all but hidden beneath a thick, neatly-trimmed moustache.

I just nodded.

'Follow me.'

I instantly felt uncomfortable around this man. As I followed him through thick doors that locked behind us, my heart was hammering, and it took all my willpower not to refuse to go any further. As we walked, the guard – I supposed that that's what he was – pointed out places that I would need to know, including the toilets, showers, dining room and, lastly, the room where I would sleep. I hesitate to call it 'my bedroom'. It was small, with three identical cots laid side-by-side. The guard showed me to my bed and told me to place the few belongings I had on the bedspread.

For now, I was the only kid in the room. I was grateful for this, because I had brought my stuffed turtle and realised, now, how inappropriate it would seem. When he saw my teddy bear, the man's moustache twitched but he didn't smile.

'I might … ah … take that,' he said.

I just nodded.

When he was gone, I looked around the room. If this place really *was* a jail for kids, like Kelly said, it seemed strange that they hadn't secured the windows, particularly when we were only one floor up.

For the next few days, I spoke to nobody, not even the two boys I shared a room with. They were older than me by at least a couple of years, and could have bullied me if they'd wanted to, but they didn't. They didn't seem interested in me at all.

One thing that made the transition to the Centre easier was the routine. We ate at designated times, showered when told, had some recreation and education time throughout the day then went to sleep when our lights were turned off.

The best thing that happened, in my first week, was when I attended my first cooking class, where our instructor taught us to make pizzas from scratch. Under his tutelage, we rolled our dough, spun our bases and chose our toppings before sliding our trays into the large ovens. The only pizzas I'd eaten were with Dad, when we'd visited Pizza Hut on special occasions, so I was excited to see what my own creation would taste like. And I wasn't disappointed.

A couple of days later, we were told that we would all be competing in the annual Baltara Swimming Carnival, which was scheduled for later in the week. It sounded like fun. I enjoyed competition of any type, and looked forward to having the chance to test my swimming skills against the other boys.

When the morning of the swimming carnival arrived, I wolfed down my cornflakes, changed into my shorts, and waited in the marshalling area where I would receive my instructions for the remainder of the morning.

Since taking up residence, I had learned that Baltara was divided into different sections. Mine was called Kinta, and was reserved for kids who had committed petty crimes. The other sections were reserved for kids who had committed more serious crimes or had diagnosed mental health issues. The swimming carnival was one of the few occasions when all of the kids were encouraged to mix.

The first half of the day went really well. The sun was shining and, for the most part, I could almost forget I was locked in a facility without choice. I competed in as many races as I could and did quite well in some.

After lunch, we were permitted some free time. It was nice to just splash around and enjoy the cool water. I was paddling on my back, staring into the blue sky, when one of the older inmates stepped into my line of sight. I was about to stand up when he grabbed my head and pushed me under water.

I didn't know this kid, but he was big and strong and no matter how hard I struggled and kicked, I couldn't escape his grasp. I expected help. It never came.

That day, I learned that running out of breath is one of the most frightening and horrible feelings. As I sank further under the water, my lungs felt like they were about explode and I screamed, bubbles streaming upwards from my lips.

When all my air was gone, I felt myself blacking out. Finally, the terror left me, and I felt calm. My arms and legs went limp.

Just then, the kid pulled my head up and out of the water, and my lungs began to work again. As I sucked in breath after breath, all I could hear was laughter. I looked over my attacker's shoulder and saw the guard with the potbelly standing poolside, hands on his knees as he laughed.

When I was able to climb out of the pool, I walked shakily to a spot where I was surrounded by other boys closer to my age, and lay on the warm concrete. Although I wanted to be strong, I couldn't stop the tears flowing, and hid my head beneath one of my arms.

To my relief, either nobody noticed, or nobody cared, because the boys left me alone until it was time to head back inside.

From that point on, I changed. I was angry. In the weeks that followed, I took on the role of the tough guy, responding to any real or imagined slight with fierce aggression. I prayed it would be enough for people to just leave me alone. The one light in the darkness was cooking class, where I spent as much time as I was allowed meticulously preparing my food, then savouring every bite.

The longer I stayed, the more the routine wore on me. The days felt never-ending, the activities boring and repetitive. Sometimes, I watched the guards and wondered whether our boredom and loneliness were not just an unfortunate consequence of our conditions but were the intended outcome.

Following my near-drowning, I struggled to sleep. Every night, I lay in bed, wishing that by some miracle Dad would show up, perhaps standing on the grass below my window. I thought about how high up we were, and figured that I could make the jump without too much damage. But this wasn't a foster home in the suburbs. This was a secure facility.

One night, the loneliness became too much. I had learned to cry quietly, so as not to attract the attention of the other boys or the guards, but this night my crying turned quickly to sobs.

It was too loud. I knew it. The other boys shushed me, but I couldn't stop.

I jumped with fright as the door to our room swung open and hit the concrete wall with a *thud*. I pushed my face, now wet with tears, deeper into my pillow, hoping the guard was not here for me, but knowing he was. I felt a strong hand grab the back of my pyjama top and pull me to my feet. Then the guard dragged me across the floor and out of the door by the collar of my pyjamas.

'Please!' I said, though my sobs. 'Please just let me stay in my room!'

The guard lifted me to my feet and pushed me in front of him, then said, 'Walk!'

My breath hitching, I did what I was told, placing one foot carefully in front of the other: left … right … left. Then, as I lifted my right leg, I felt a flash of pain in the middle of my back and the breath was forced out of my lungs.

As I fell forward, I thought of the day Emile had hit me with the rock, the way I'd fallen from the swing, the breath knocked out of me. But this time I wasn't falling backwards, I was falling forwards.

I raised my hands, but I was too slow. My cheek hit the linoleum floor and I lay motionless as the pain jolted through me, wave after wave.

I was barely conscious of being pulled to my feet, but suddenly I felt the guard's arm around my neck. I remembered the feeling of being under the water with the bigger boy holding me down and fought the guard's arm, but again it was a case of somebody bigger and stronger forcing me to submit.

I fought as best I could as he dragged me backwards down the corridor and into another room, this one with a tiled floor. As my bare feet slid across the tiles, I realised where we were: the shower room. I had just begun to wonder why we were there when the guard tossed me onto the ground and punched me beneath my solar plexus. I vomited and pissed myself simultaneously, then felt a crushing shame that rivalled the pain.

'You're fucking disgusting!' the guard said, flicking vomit off his usually-immaculate shirt. Then he spun the tap, dowsing me with the bitterly cold water.

Immediately my teeth began to chatter. Then the guard was turning the water off and picking me up by the arm, leading me back through the shower room and down the hallway to my room.

Once inside, he said nothing. He didn't have to. Before leaving, however, he spun me around and looked into my eyes. I peered back into his eyes and saw no glee, no anger. I saw nothing.

The days that followed were uneventful. I kept my head down and hardly said a word to anyone. Inside, I grew more hopeless as I felt like I would never get to hear what had become of my sisters or my dad. In particular, I worried about Kelly. I knew she could handle herself, but I hated the thought of her being in a place like Baltara. I wondered whether she thought about me, then told myself to stop wondering because it was only making things worse.

One night, I heard my two roommates whispering. I turned my back, pretending not to listen … wishing I could block out their words. They were clearly planning something. A couple of days later, I would learn what it was when, just after lights out, four other boys snuck into our room. Clearly, they had been quiet enough to get past the guard without attracting his attention. Now, they revealed a rope made of bedsheets.

Just like a prison break in a movie, they tied the sheets to the leg of one of the beds – not mine, after I pleaded with them not to involve me – and began to climb out the window one-by-one.

With the others already safely on the ground outside, the last boy turned to me and said, 'Peter, wanna come?' I hadn't even known he knew my name.

I shook my head.

The boy nodded, climbed out the window, and was gone.

I rolled onto my side and stared at the wall, imagining the boys running across the grass, to freedom.

The next morning, as could be expected, the halls of Kinta were filled with commotion as the guards on duty realised that six boys were missing. It didn't take long to realise how they had escaped. I was escorted into the main guard's office and questioned extensively, but I stuck to my story: I had been asleep and hadn't heard or seen anything.

After being warned several times not to lie or I too would be punished, the guards let me go. They had no choice. With all the excitement, the usual guards had been pulled in for questioning, and Kinta was being managed – at least for the day – by more senior staff.

In the dayroom, I found a book and sat in a corner, trying to occupy myself with a story of a mystical battle involving dwarves and giants, but it was little use. After a little while, another boy who I occasionally played with sat down next to me. He shook his head. 'What I don't get, Pete,' he said, 'You hate it here, right?'

I nodded. Of course I hated it. We all did.

'So why didn't you go with them?' the kid asked, 'When you had the chance?'

'I was asleep,' I said, and went back to reading my book.

It took three days for the boys to be found and brought back to the facility. Now, they weren't allowed to live in Kinta. They were considered 'high risk', and would have to live in another wing … somewhere even worse.

*

A couple of weeks later, the escape was old news. Nobody seemed to care what I had or hadn't known anymore. I had been enjoying my relative anonymity. I had new roommates, but we never spoke to each other. I didn't even know their names, and they didn't know mine.

Having finished breakfast, I headed to the shower block. It was open plan and run down, the showers shuddering as the water ran, the tiles cracked underfoot. Like everyone else, I'd heard the stories about the showers. I was relieved to see that the place was deserted, and stood under the lukewarm water for only as long as it took me to soap myself and wash away the suds.

It was as I was finishing up that I heard a commotion outside, and turned to see three older boys drag a skinny kid in by his hair. They threw him in the shower at the opposite end of the block to mine and turned on the cold tap. He squealed – the kind of squeal that indicates shock rather than pain, so it must water must have been cold. I turned my own shower off as quietly as I could and grabbed my towel, wrapping it around my waist.

The boy struggled violently, but his attackers held him down with ease.

I turned away. I could still see what was happening out of the corner of my eye, but I didn't want to be seen to be openly looking in case I became the bullies' next target.

I jumped as I heard a slap, then several thuds. Somebody laughed while somebody else sobbed.

'God, I hate this place,' I thought.

Later that same morning, one of the guards came to collect me from class. I knew immediately why I had been singled out. They would ask me what I'd seen in the showers that morning and I'd have to lie and say I didn't see anything.

Oh, well. I was getting used to the lies.

But when I entered the guards' station, the only person waiting for me was a woman I didn't recognise. She had short, spiky hair and held out a hand towards me. I shook it; an old instinct. 'I'm Cathy,' she said.

Cathy told me to sit down. Then she pulled up one of the green plastic chairs and sat down opposite me, surprisingly close. She was smiling. I felt an immediate sense of distrust at that smile. But there was something about her eyes … something soft … and kind.

It's amazing how quickly you can forget kindness exists.

Excitedly, Cathy said, 'Peter, we've found you somewhere to stay. It's only temporary, but it will get you out of here. Would you like that?'

Until that moment, I hadn't realised how much tension I'd been holding in my body. I almost collapsed and was glad that she'd told me to sit. Then I realised her hand was on my shoulder, squeezing me gently through my t-shirt.

I had to fight back the urge to cry.

'Thank you,' I whispered. 'Thank you.'

And yet, despite my relief at getting out of Baltara, I felt a sharp tug of disappointment that the person sitting opposite me, their hand on my shoulder, was not my Dad.

# Chapter 10

# THE WEIGHT OF NEW BEGINNINGS

On the morning I was due to be collected, I woke up early, showered, and tried to eat breakfast, but the butterflies in my tummy didn't allow for much food. Then I went back to my room, packed what little I owned into my small blue nylon bag, and sat on the end of my bed until it was time for the guard to escort me to the front office.

It was around 10am when the guard with the moustache finally came. He checked my bag, then motioned for me to walk ahead of him. The whole time, I kept expecting to feel the jab of his club in my back, but it never came.

In the office, I saw Cathy again. She was sitting behind a desk, with a neat stack of paperwork in front of her. She had already begun filling it out. She thanked the guard, who gave me a quick grin before he disappeared through the doorway and walked, whistling, back into Kinta. As his whistle died away, I felt like I could breathe again. Cathy asked questions, which I did my best to answer, and she filled out form after form. Then finally she told me we were done, stood up, and told me to follow her.

I still remember the feel of the warmth of the sun on my skin as we stepped outside that morning. A light breeze caused the branches of the nearby trees to sway and I took a moment to just stand still, breathing in and out slowly. During my stay, I had spent plenty of time outside – rec time, they called it – but this was entirely different. Suddenly, I knew I was never coming back.

When we reached the carpark, Cathy opened the back door of her neat sedan and flashed me another one of her smiles. I was getting almost used to them by this point. 'Climb in,' she said.

For the next forty-five minutes or so, we travelled without saying much. I stared out the window, watching the houses flash by. They all looked wonderful. Real houses with real families inside. And one of them was waiting for me.

Finally, Cathy turned on her indicator and pulled up to the curb in front of a large red brick house. Its lawn was perfectly manicured, and rose bushes of different colours lined the pathway to the front door. All were in full bloom.

Before we got out, Cathy unbuckled her seatbelt and turned around, her expression more serious than I'd seen it up until this point. She was holding a large file.

Cathy explained that the family we were going to meet had only agreed to look after me for a short period of time. I asked how long, and she said, 'That's up to them, I'm afraid. We have no choice but to … to take their lead.'

I'd heard my dad talk about probation enough to know what she was hinting at.

Her voice suddenly lighter, Cathy opened the file and read from one of the pages. According to her notes, the family had two boys, one younger than me, the other older. I listened with a mixture of fear and excitement. Then she closed the file and smiled again, wider this time but a little less convincingly.

I smiled back.

'Ready?' Cathy asked.

I nodded.

We climbed out of the car and walked up the winding brick pathway until we stood outside a large white door with a brass handle. Cathy raised the knocker and let it fall. I heard the knock echo through the house.

It didn't take long before the door swung open and a short, round man stood in front of us, wearing a brown cardigan, and glasses that sat at the end of his nose, the lenses below his eyes. I was still wondering why somebody would wear glasses if they didn't need to look through then all the time when he held out a hand. I shook it, and was surprised at how soft it felt. Not like Dad's.

'Hello there,' the man said. 'You must be Peter. My name is Tim.'

I nodded, silently.

'Come in and you can meet everyone.'

Tim ushered us into the cleanest living room I had ever seen, where the rest of the family sat side-by-side on a white, overstuffed couch. Tim introduced me to his wife, Helen, and his children, Robert and Matthew. Helen nodded to me, demurely, while both boys just stared.

For the next few minutes, Cathy took Tim and Helen through the necessary paperwork, while I perched on the edge of a chair, opposite the couch. Even with my eyes lowered, I could feel Robert and Matthew still watching me. None of us said anything.

I was happy to have escaped Baltara, but this place hardly felt welcoming.

Half an hour later, Cathy collected her things, stood up and told me she would be in touch soon. She farewelled the family, then headed back out the front door and down the path to her car. As the door closed behind her, Helen offered to take me on a tour. I walked slightly behind her, breathing in the faint musk of her perfume. It smelled of vanilla with a hint of lavender.

Beyond the living room, which I had already seen, there was a dining room with a large, mahogany table that gleamed in the light filtered through sheer lace curtains. Beyond that, with French doors offering access to a large, immaculately-maintained back garden, was the kitchen. Unlike the kitchens I had seen before, there was nothing on the benches. Within a purpose-built recess was a glass-fronted device, smaller than a conventional oven.

Helen saw the focus of my attention and smiled slightly. 'Have you seen one of those before?' she asked. 'It's a microwave.' When I didn't respond, she elaborated, 'It heats food or drinks … really quickly.'

From somewhere behind me, I heard one of the boys snort with laughter and saw Helen shoot them a look. Then she said, 'Let me show you your room.'

Upstairs, I glanced into a spotless family bathroom, and both boys' rooms, which looked like mirror images, both blue with a white, single bed, a matching set of drawers, and a small bookshelf lined with books. At the end of the hall was my room. I stood in the doorway for a moment, struck by the difference between this room and the rooms I was used to sleeping in. Even before Baltara, I hadn't had my own room in years. There was a single bed in the centre of the room, and a set of drawers against one wall. Like the other boys, I, too, had a bookshelf, but it was empty.

'Do you like to read, Peter?' Helen asked.

I nodded, thinking about the voracious appetite for books I had developed at Baltara.

'You can borrow some books from Matthew and Robert,' Helen said. 'I've been trying to implement a read-before-bed policy, but they have been less than keen. Unless it's about cricket, they don't want to know about it.'

Finally, she squeezed my shoulder. I glanced at her hand, and she withdrew it, appearing slightly embarrassed. I wished I hadn't made her feel bad about touching me. I was still thinking about this, and wondering whether I should say something, when she asked me if I needed anything else. I told her no thank you, and she said she would leave me to unpack.

My clothes consisted of a set of pyjamas and two sets of clothes other than the ones I was wearing. They all fit in a single drawer. Aside from that, the only thing I owned was Tom the Turtle. I had never unpacked him at Baltara. Now, I removed him carefully from the bottom of my bag and hugged him to my chest as I sat down on the bed. My bed, I reminded myself. After a few quiet minutes on my own, I lay Tom on my pillow and left the room. I pulled the door closed quietly, then walked to the end of the hall and down the winding staircase.

On the ground floor, I heard shouts and laughter, muted by the glass of the French doors. I walked into the kitchen and watched the boys playing in the backyard.

'You should join them,' Helen said.

I turned my head to find her standing in the kitchen, sipping a cup of tea. She had been watching the boys through the window above the sink. 'I'm sure they'd love to have another … friend … to play with.'

After a moment's hesitation, I stepped outside and felt my breath catch in my throat.

The biggest backyard my family had ever owned had been in Sunshine. Being a rental property, it hadn't been given consistent care, and was mostly dirt with just a few tufts of lawn poking up obstinately here and there. Every time a new shoot emerged, it became fodder for our rabbits, which had begun as a pair but quickly multiplied until they were underfoot, threatening to trip me up when I headed to the thunderbox during the night.

This yard was at least twice the length of the one in Sunshine, and many times the width. It had a swing set, a sandpit, and even a trampoline. To my young eyes, it looked more like a park than a private garden. I couldn't believe other kids actually lived like this.

The younger boy, Robert, was playing in the sandpit, so I went over and sat on the edge, careful not to touch any of the toys scattered through the sand. After a minute or so, without looking up, Robert pushed a large yellow tip truck in my direction. Leaning down, I turned it around and pushed it back. We continued our game for a few minutes. Then, without warning, Robert stood up and ran to the back door, shouting, 'Mum, I'm bored!'

'Why don't you ask Peter what he wants to do?' Helen asked. 'He would probably love to see all your toys.'

For a moment, Robert stared at me dubiously. Then he shrugged. 'Want to play with my toys?' he asked.

I nodded.

In his room, Robert slid a storage box out from underneath his bed and revealed hundreds of plastic figurines: *Star Wars, Mask, He-Man.* Now, I was in heaven.

We spent the rest of the afternoon playing with the figurines outside in the sun. Sometimes, we imagined that they were part of a scene and gave them dialogue. Other times, we made them wrestle each other, moving them in slow motion and making the sound effects of punches and kicks with our lips pursed together. Even Matthew joined in with that, using his favourite figure, Skeletor. But he was too rough, and insisted on Skeletor winning every match. When he made Robert cry, I considered saying something, but I remembered what Cathy had said about my probation.

The sun was low in the sky when Helen poked her head through the back door and told us to wash up for dinner. We headed to the bathroom, where we washed our hands. The soap smelled like lavender, and made my hands feel soft. I tried not to let the other boys see how impressed I was with everything, knowing that it would only mark me as an outsider.

Despite my attempt not to dawdle, both boys left the bathroom before me.

In the hallway once more, I noticed for the first time the rich smells wafting through the house, and realised how hungry I was. I eagerly headed towards the dining room, where I found Tim and the two boys already seated at the table, while Helen placed a large, ornate dish on a placemat in the middle of the table. I reached for the chair next to Robert's and was just about to sit when Tim stopped me, a hand placed lightly against my chest.

'Not here, Peter,' he said.

He motioned past both boys. I followed his gaze and noticed that a small blue plastic table and matching chair had been placed in the corner of the room. For a moment, I was confused. I looked at the boys. Robert wouldn't meet my gaze, but Matthew was smirking. Then I looked from back at Tim and saw the same expression.

Without a word, I walked to the little table and sat down. I felt stupid now, for believing – even for a moment – that I could ever be accepted in a place like this.

Then Helen placed a piece of steaming hot shepherd's pie in front of me. I looked up to see her smiling, a genuine smile that made me want to cry.

'Thank you,' I mumbled.

'You're welcome, Peter,' Helen said. As she had earlier, she put a hand on my shoulder. This time she left it there for a few moments.

The shepherd's pie tasted as good as it looked. Sitting with my back to the family allowed me to close my eyes and savour each bite.

After dinner, I placed my knife and fork together in the centre of my plate and turned around. Tim and the boys had already finished their meal, and Helen had served them each a bowl of ice cream. Noticing that I had finished, she placed another bowl in front of her and began to dig into the ice cream with the metal scoop. When she glanced at Tim, a peculiar expression crossed her face. From where I was sitting, I couldn't see his face, but I saw the tiny shake of his head.

In the kitchen, a few minutes later, I found Helen standing at the sink. I handed her my plate and thanked her for dinner. 'You're welcome, Peter,' she said, then added, 'You'd better get ready for bed.'

As I climbed the stairs, I heard the opening strains of *Hey, Hey, it's Saturday*, a show I had always enjoyed.

In the upstairs bathroom, I locked the door, then brushed my teeth and used the toilet without fear of being interrupted. After climbing into bed, I thought about the regret on Helen's face as she had put the ice cream scoop away without serving me. I felt bad for her, and wished I could tell her what a relief it was to be here. I was still thinking about Helen when I fell asleep.

The next morning, I woke up feeling more well-rested than I had in months. I sat up and saw the sun peering through the window. Then I felt a light pressure on my feet and looked at the end of the bed, where a book had been left for me. I knew immediately that it had come from Helen. She must have taken it out of one of the other boys' bedrooms and left it here during the night.

*The Neverending Story*, by Michael Ende.

Unlike the books at Baltara, which were donated by the local community and abused by the few boys who borrowed them, this book looked like it had never been read. I opened it, sniffed the pages, and began to read.

In the story, a boy named Bastian became entwined in the most amazing adventures. As I read, I fantasised that I was Bastian and would be whisked away from real life to become a hero in a mystical world.

As the full sun made its way through the window, somebody knocked on my door.

'Come in,' I said, feeling almost silly at the formality of the words. I couldn't remember anybody ever knocking on my bedroom door before.

'Good morning, Peter.' Helen stepped into the room.

When she saw me reading, Helen said, 'You found it.'

'I love it,' I said.

Helen beamed. 'Ready for breakfast?'

Nodding, I climbed out of bed and pulled my covers back up to the pillow, then followed her downstairs.

Without being asked, I made my way to my little blue table, where I happily ate a bowl of cereal, followed by toast with butter and jam.

Later that day, Tim and Helen drove us to a local shopping mall. We parked in a large, open-air carpark. Helen had told me that Robert and Matthew needed some new school clothes. Neither of the boys seemed to care about buying clothes, however. They spent the drive chattering excitedly about going to the movies and buying popcorn. In the front passenger seat, Tim was scanning a newspaper, reading out the titles of movies as well as the occasional review. I wondered whether we would, indeed, go to the cinema. I hadn't been in several years, and felt my tummy rumble at the prospect of eating popcorn.

When we arrived at the shopping mall, all five of us wandered down gleaming corridors filled with shops. I found it hard to avoid the oncoming crowd, and had to dance left and right to avoid colliding with shoppers, their hands filled with bags emblazoned with the names of shops I had never heard of.

As I followed the family, I watched Tim. He didn't seem like a bad person, but when Robert tried to take his hand, he shook off the grasp, saying, 'No. You're a big boy now, remember?'

Dad was never like that. He never told any of us kids not to give him a kiss or a cuddle in public. And he often told me he loved me.

At that moment, I wanted desperately to know that he was okay.

I admired the precision with which Helen found items for Robert and Matthew. After leaving Country Road, she explained apologetically that my caseworker, Cathy, would buy my clothes. I was about to assure her that I didn't need anything when Tim said, 'He's fine, Helen. He's understands. Don't you, Peter?'

I nodded at Tim, then at Helen.

After shopping, we caught an escalator up one floor to where the cinema was located. By this time, Robert and Matthew were jumping around in anticipation.

Finally, as the boys raced ahead and Tim sauntered ahead in an attempt to catch up, Helen took a deep breath. Then she placed her shopping bags on the ground and knelt down. 'It's just Tim and the boys going to the movies today, Peter. But, lucky you, you get to stay with me.'

For a moment, I felt disappointed. Then I looked at Tim and felt slightly glad. As he and the boys stood in line for their cinema tickets, Helen held out her hand and I took it. I was amazed at how soft and warm her skin felt against mine.

Minutes later, we were sitting at a small coffee shop with a view of a grand piano, where a man in a tuxedo was playing a jaunty tune. Helen held the menu out towards me. I took it from her hands and glanced at the glossy images of all different types of cakes.

'Choose anything you want,' Helen said, then lowered her voice to a whisper. 'But don't tell the boys. They've had plenty of treats already, and Tim is meant to be on a diet.'

For some reason, this made her laugh. For the first time, I noticed that she had a dimple in each cheek.

When my chocolate mud cake arrived, I greedily shovelled forkfuls into my mouth. I was finishing up when Helen touched my hand and said, 'Peter?'

I looked up.

Her expression was serious. In a soft voice, she told me that my dad had been moved to Fremantle in Western Australia to face his charges.

I had so many questions. Why Western Australia? Why so far away? When would he get out?

Helen couldn't answer any of these questions, but her expression was soft and I knew that, for as long as I stayed with her, I would have a friend. I asked whether she knew where any of my brothers or sisters had ended up, and she said she hadn't been told.

We spent the next hour just wandering around the mall and continuing to chat. We wended our way past the glittering stores, and – too soon – I realised we were back at the cinema. As we approached, Helen gave my hand a squeeze, then let it go before Tim or the boys could see.

As soon as they saw their mum, Matthew and Robert wanted to tell her all about the movie. It sounded like they'd had a great time, and I felt genuinely happy for them.

We were on our way out of the store when I caught a glimpse of a tall man in blue jeans and a white t-shirt. He was still a long way off, but I would know that walk anywhere.

Dad!

I ran down the hallway, as fast as I could, to where the man had been standing only moments earlier, but he wasn't there. I looked around frantically. My breathing was shallow and tears welled in my eyes.

When Tim, Helen and the boys caught up to me, Tim grabbed my shoulder, his fingers biting into my flesh through my t-shirt. 'What the hell is wrong with you?' he yelled.

I didn't answer him. I couldn't. My dad had been here, only moments ago. I didn't want to lose him again.

I tried to run, to search for him again, but Tim grabbed my other shoulder. His face red, chest puffed out, he was clearly about to say something else when Helen placed a hand on her husband's forearm.

She stepped between us, breaking her husband's grip, then knelt down and looked me in the eye. 'Peter, what happened?'

Suddenly, I couldn't help it. I felt the running tears down my cheeks and threw my arms around her. 'I just ... my dad ... he was right here!' I protested.

'Shhhh,' Helen said, holding me, stroking my hair. 'Shush now.'

Suddenly, I felt a rough hand close around mine, and somebody jerked me backwards. Tim was dragging me in the direction of the large double-doors at the end of the hallway, muttering, 'What a bloody embarrassment!'

When we got back to the house, Tim sent me straight to my room. Almost instantly, I heard raised voices, and knew that Tim and Helen were arguing. Worse than that, I knew that it was about me.

As I lay in bed, I wondered whether that could really have been Dad back at the shopping mall. Helen had said he was in Fremantle. I didn't know exactly how far away that was, but I knew it was a long way. He'd escaped before. Maybe he'd done it again, and come here looking for me …?

I must have slept, because the next thing I was aware of was Helen sitting on the side of my bed. She asked whether I was okay, and I told her I was.

After she left, I picked up *The Neverending Story* and read it for another hour, glad to be transported once more to the safety of the world of Fantastica. Sometime later, Helen brought my dinner to my room. Once I'd finished it, I rose and brushed my teeth, then went back to bed and turned off my bedside lamp.

For a while, I lay still and silent in the dark. Then, just as I felt myself drifting off to sleep, I heard a soft knock. I looked up. It felt late. I had heard the other boys go to bed at least an hour ago.

Then I heard another knock.

It wasn't coming from my bedroom door. It was coming from the window.

Sitting up, my heart pounding, I crossed the room and peered through the glass, down into the thick foliage of the side garden. For a few moments, I saw nothing. Then, as my eyes finally grew accustomed to the darkness, I saw the man. He wore blue jeans, a white t-shirt, and a wide grin.

Dad!

# Chapter 11

# THE BREADWINNER

I closed my eyes and wiped away the tears with the back of my hand, sure that, when I opened them again, Dad would be gone. But, as I took a step closer to the window, he was still standing there.

I was going home!

Grabbing Tom the Turtle off the bed, I threw him in my bag, piled my few items of clothing on top of him and slid the sash window up, feeling the cool night air on my face. For a moment, I considered taking *The Neverending Story* with me. I was almost sure Helen wouldn't mind, and it's not like either of the boys would notice. But it didn't feel right, so I left it where it lay, at the end of my bed. Then I climbed out the window backwards and lowered my legs, fingers tight on the wooden window-frame. I hung there briefly, the night air cold through my pyjamas. Then Dad said, 'Go!' and I released my grasp.

For a moment, I felt weightless. Then my feet hit the ground, and dad's hands were on my back, keeping me upright. I whirled around and held him as tight as I could. He felt thinner – more wiry – but he was still strong. Still Dad.

He kissed my forehead, then held my face in his hands for a moment before he said, 'Need to hurry.'

I nodded. There would be time for questions later.

We ran away from the redbrick house, to where Dad had parked, in a dark spot away from the glowing streetlights. He turned the key, looked back at the house, and pressed the pedal to the floor. We took off with a roar, and I was suddenly laughing. Dad looked at me. I had never seen him smile so wide.

We didn't slow down until we reached the freeway. Then Dad merged into traffic and kept his eyes partly on the road ahead and partly on the rear-view mirror. Seeing him watch his mirror so carefully made me feel nervous.

Finally, Dad seemed to relax, and asked me whether I'd been well looked after at Baltara. I told him a few things, avoiding anything I thought might make him feel guilty about not being there. I asked about my brother and sisters. He said they were okay, and assured me that we'd all be together again soon.

When we reached Melbourne's CBD, Dad pulled to the side of the road. He told me to grab my things and climbed out of the car. I had to run to catch up. Above me towered the State Library. I looked up at its grey-green façade, its deep shadows, and couldn't help but feel afraid for a moment.

'Aren't you taking the car?' I asked.

'Nah!' Dad said, with a quick grin. 'Needed a change.'

'Where are we going?' I asked.

'I've organised somewhere for us to stay," he said. 'It isn't far.'

We continued to walk down Swanston Street, then waited for a tram to pass. When I shivered with cold, Dad put his arm around me. Even after I was warm, I kept shaking every so often so that he would hold me tighter.

Finally, we passed Spencer Street Station. Even at night, there were lots of people, and I could hear the rattle of trains arriving and departing within. We walked along Spencer Street until we came to a brick high-rise. 'This is it,' Dad announced. Then he looked down at the ground and I saw a strange expression cross his face. Embarrassment, perhaps, or shame. He added, 'I'm not gonna lie, Pete. It's no palace.'

Already, a knot of dread was beginning to form in the pit of my stomach.

Dad held open one of two large glass doors. Even before I stepped inside, I was hit with the smell of stale piss. I tried holding my nose, then breathing through my mouth, but it did no good. It felt like the smell was burning my nostrils, the back of my throat. I looked around a dimly lit foyer, at several old men slumped on worn armchairs. Some were talking, while others stared off into space. A sign above the reception desk read Gordon House.

Dad approached the desk. The booking clerk asked Dad to fill out a form, which he did. As he took the form from Dad, the clerk gave me a glance, then fixed his gaze at Dad. 'This is no place for a kid, mate,' he said. When Dad didn't answer, he shook his head, sighed, and signed the form, which he placed in a filing cabinet beside him. Then he took a key out of a draw and handed it to Dad.

We entered the elevators and Dad let me press the button for the eighth floor. The elevator rattled its way upwards. I imagined it stopping, the overhead light blinking off, the rope snapping and the little metal box plunging to the ground. But of course, it didn't happen. Eventually, it came to a sudden halt and the doors slid open with a screech of metal-on-metal.

At the end of a dingy hallway, we found Room 822. Dad slid the key into the lock. I slipped my hand into his. He glanced at me for a moment and gave me one of his quick it'll-be-okay grins. I grinned back, but my smile faded the moment he looked away.

Dad opened the door. The room was only just big enough to accommodate two small beds with a small wardrobe between them. 'You can put your stuff in there,' Dad said, motioning to my backpack. Only now did I realise that he had no bag.

Dutifully, I took off my bag. I unzipped it and took out my stuffed turtle.

'You still have that thing!' Dad said, laughing. 'Good old Tom.'

'Of course,' I said. 'He's part of the family.'

*

When I woke the next morning, Dad was sitting up in bed, reading the newspaper. He must have left the room earlier and come back without waking me up. 'Hungry?' he asked.

'Starving,' I said, surprised to find that this was the case, despite the stale smell of our room.

Downstairs, we joined what seemed like more than a hundred men who congregated in orderly lines, waiting for breakfast to be served. Most of them looked lost and unhappy.

As we waited to be served eggs and beans from the bain-marie, Dad squeezed my shoulder. I looked up at him and he said, 'Stay close, alright? And don't talk to anybody unless I'm with you.'

While I ate and tried to ignore the acrid smell of the place, I sneaked a few glances at the men seated around us – their long, coarse beards and hair, their stained jackets and coats, their weathered faces, and knew there was no way I'd let him out of my sight in this place.

Later, I would learn that Gordon House was a homeless shelter. Although the place housed women as well, I didn't see any during our stay. I was the only child.

The next few days passed without incident. Each morning, we got up and had breakfast. Then I followed Dad around. I never asked him when we would would be leaving. I trusted he had a plan. We spent most of our time in the large lounge, furnished in thick padded chairs, covered in a brown velvet-like material. While Dad talked and laughed with the other men, I played Galaga at twenty cents a pop. Every time I finished, and the little spaceship went into its tailspin of death, I returned to Dad and waited until he handed me another coin.

In our room one night, Dad told me how he'd escaped from Fremantle Prison. He'd faked an illness that meant the prison doctors scheduled him to be taken to hospital. It was after he'd been taken up to the ward, between an MRI and an ECG, that the doctor left him alone for just a moment. With the guards in the hallway outside the room, Dad climbed out the window. He was only one storey off the ground, and had jumped down into the hospital grounds before stealing a car from the parking lot. He laughed while he told the story. I laughed too.

After lights out, however, my happiness quickly faded away. It was replaced with an old worry: somebody knocking on the door, taking Dad away, then taking me away too. To another family. Or another boys' home.

The next day, we spent some time walking around the city. We didn't buy anything, and it struck me that Dad had no money. When I'd been playing Galaga and asking him for coins, he'd begun by tossing them to me with a smile, but – as the days wore on – he'd seemed less enthusiastic about parting with them. Now I understood why. I knew better than to raise the issue with him directly; he was too proud for that. Instead, when I saw a boy selling newspapers, I said, 'I could do that, Dad.'

For a moment, he watched him, his lips pressed firmly together. Then his expression appeared to brighten and he said, 'Too right.'

Grabbing my hand, he walked me to the distribution warehouse of the Herald, which was published each afternoon, and down a concrete ramp, into a large and busy space, where people were quickly going about their tasks. We followed signs to the administration window, where Dad informed the man behind the counter that I wanted to be a paperboy. Without asking why I wasn't at school, the man told me to come back the next day for a trial. 'Twelve sharp,' he said, as we walked away.

At 11:55am the next day, as we approached the warehouse, I let go of Dad's hand and said, 'I'll be alright. See you back here at 5:30.'

With a look of mild surprise, Dad nodded. 'Whatever you say, Pete.'

A few minutes later, the same man who'd taken my details the day before showed me to a stack of papers. 'These are yours,' he said. 'And you'll need this, too.' He handed me a small leather pouch attached to a belt. 'You can put your money in there. And if you need more papers, just look for the truck. They'll be able to re-stock you.'

'Where do I go?" I asked.

'Wherever you like," he said. 'But the best spots are near the train stations. Flinders Street, Spencer Street. Parliament.'

I grabbed my stack of papers and ran as fast as I could considering the load I was carrying. I headed for Flinders Street Station, knowing I had to be quick if I wanted to get the best spot. I was almost there when I had the strange feeling I was being followed.

A block later, I whirled around and saw Dad following a few meters behind me. He tried hiding behind a businessman in a navy suit, but it was no use. Holding up his hands, he began to laugh.

'Dad!' I yelled. 'What are you doing?'

'Sorry, kid,' Dad said, walking closer. He was still laughing softly. 'Just had to make sure you were safe. I don't wanna lose you again.'

As he looked down at me, I saw pride in his eyes and felt my cheeks get hot with embarrassment. I couldn't help smiling, but I insisted he leave me to do my job alone. Finally – a little reluctantly – he agreed.

A few minutes later, I found a spot right near the steps that led up to Flinders Street Station, beneath the clocks that showed passengers what time their trains would leave. Selling papers as the men and women stopped on the steps was as easy as holding out a paper, taking the money they handed me, and occasionally giving out some change.

I'd been there for no more than ten minutes, and was already halfway through my stock, when an older man came up, clearly agitated. 'Hey, you little bastard,' he yelled, 'this is my spot!'

'Who says?' I asked, selling another paper.

'Ask anyone!' the guy said. 'Go find somewhere else!"

As another businessman took a paper out of my hand and gave me a dollar note in exchange, I went to give him change, but the new arrival knocked the coins out of my hand. They jingled as they bounced down the steps and were lost under the feet of passersby.

I was just about to shout 'Hey!' when I sensed – rather than saw – something in my periphery. I glanced to my left and saw Dad marching up the Flinders Street steps. I knew what his next move would be, and – to both our surprise – I stepped between him and my rival salesman, shaking my head.

Seeing my determination, Dad stopped, his face red, his chest rising and falling in anger. Turning away from him, I looked up at the man and made my voice hard, just like I'd heard Dad do so many times. 'I was here first,' I said. 'I found the best spot, and I'm. Not. Moving.'

For a few moments, the man just watched me, considering his options. Then I spoke again. 'I'll tell you what: how about I keep this spot today, you have it tomorrow, I have it the day after that. We share it. And if anybody else tries to take it, we both run them off.'

At this moment, a businessman tried to buy one of my papers. Instead, I directed him to the older salesman, who made the sale without ever looking away from me. Then he shook his head, smiling ruefully. 'Ok, kid,' he said. 'You've got a deal.'

A few minutes later, I took a moment's break from selling papers to look for my dad, but I couldn't see him. I hoped he was really gone this time. That day, the hours seemed to race by, and I had to re-stock several times. Whenever I did, the older salesman took my spot, but dutifully moved away each time I returned. At five o'clock, I waved goodbye to him and headed back to the warehouse. I handed over my pouch, and received a small envelope with my commission for the day's sales in return.

Dad was waiting outside. Without ever looking inside the envelope, I handed it to him, and we walked back to Gordon House in a comfortable silence.

I continued to sell papers for the next couple of weeks, each day giving Dad the money to buy the few small food and personal items we needed to survive. Over dinner one night, he told me that he couldn't claim financial assistance or get a legitimate job or he might be caught. I told him not to worry – that I was happy to be earning money for us. I was proud to help and happy to do whatever was required to make sure that we could stay together. Dad eventually stopped walking me to and from the Herald, explaining that the less he was out in public, the better for us both.

One particularly busy afternoon, I finished up a few minutes late on the Flinders Street steps and was surprised to see Dad waiting for me down the bottom. He waved to me, and I traipsed down the stairs, selling my final paper just before I reached him. 'Dad,' I said, 'You wouldn't believe how many copies I sold today!'

Instead of looking happy, Dad seemed worried. I felt my own smile fade.

'Let's go,' Dad said, his voice tight. But, instead of heading back towards the warehouse, we walked down Flinders Street.

I suspected what Dad was going to do long before he asked, but his words still felt like a punch. 'Give us your takings,' he said, without looking at me.

Reluctantly, I handed him my money pouch. With nimble fingers, he removed the notes before tossing the empty pouch into a nearby bin.

'Let's go get ourselves a good feed,' Dad said.

I nodded, but felt a pang of longing at the realisation that my first real job was over.

*

A couple of days later, Dad told me he had a plan for us to make some more quick cash. 'It'll be enough to get us out of his shithole,' he said, thumping the worn mattress he sat on.

That afternoon, following his instructions, I took a small plastic bag with a towel and shorts and paid for one ticket to Melbourne Baths. I had never been inside the orange-and-cream building before. Now, I stepped through a glass door and immediately smelled chlorine and felt the heat of the pool.

Sweating, from nervousness as well as heat, I headed into the change rooms. When I was dressed in my shorts, I made my way back into the pool area.

I swam a few laps. It felt good to stretch my arms and glide through the warm water. For a little while, I could almost forget what I'd come here to do. Then I got out, dried my hair, and wrapped my towel around my waist.

There were five or six other swimmers doing laps, all men, all old. Their towels were hanging by the side of the pool. Just as Dad had told me they would, the swimmers had attached their locker keys to their towels, using the safety pin provided.

By the time I reached the change room, I had collected six towels, keys attached. Two minutes later, I had opened the corresponding lockers. Inside each was a suit and shoes. They also contained an assortment of wallets and watches. I removed everything of value, stuffing it into my plastic bag and placing my wet towel on top. Then I pulled on my pants, t-shirt and shoes.

I was leaving the locker room just as somebody noticed their towel was missing and shouted for an attendant. Adrenaline flooding my veins, I forced myself to walk – not run – past the reception desk. I thanked the attendant.

'Have a nice swim, love?' she asked.

'Yep,' I said, smiling. 'See you next time.'

Outside, I ran. I didn't stop until I had passed the Queen Victoria Market. Then I walked back to Gordon House at a brisk pace. Along the way, I took a peek inside one of the wallets without removing it from the bag. I couldn't believe how much money somebody would leave lying around for somebody else to find.

I knew Dad would be pleased.

Back at Gordon House, I met him in the common room. His eyes gleaming, he grabbed my hand and we caught the elevator back to our floor. Once in our room, he removed the cash from the wallets, counted it out, and placed the watches and other valuables in a neat pile. Then he patted me on the back. He told me that our haul was worth more than a thousand dollars. 'We can get a car now,' he said. 'That's all thanks to you, Son.'

Sitting on the edge of his bed, the loot spread out on the floor between us, Dad asked me to tell him exactly what had happened. I laughed as I described stopping to talk to the receptionist.

That night, Dad told me I deserved a treat. We left Gordon House at dusk, and walked to Pizza Hut, on the corner of Bourke and Elizabeth Streets. The smells as we entered made my stomach rumble.

We ate at a red leather booth. I served myself pizza and spaghetti Bolognese, followed by three serves of chocolate mousse. The whole time, Dad and I talked. He seemed so relaxed, and I was surprised to realise how much I'd been craving a sense of normality.

By the time we got back to Gordon House, it was after nine-thirty. We were about to get into the lift when I noticed that the only other occupant was an old, hunched man with shit-stained plaster on his right arm. I could smell him from a couple of metres away, and hid behind Dad in an attempt to distance myself from him.

The old man moved as if to hold the door, but Dad shook his head and said, 'We'll wait.'

The old man rode up alone.

We waited downstairs until the lift returned. Then we stepped in and I covered my nose, but I couldn't block out the old man's stench.

The doors were just about to close when two other men got in. I had maintained my position behind Dad, enjoying the feeling of him shielding me, and I suddenly felt his body tense. His hand was on my shoulder now, moving me gently but firmly behind him, out of sight of the men.

The doors closed, and the elevator began to climb. I peeked out from behind Dad, and saw that the two men wore overcoats. Both were burly, and one had a bald patch on the back of his skull. Finally, the elevator came to a halt and the balding man said, in a low voice, 'When we get up there, wait for my instructions.'

The other man nodded, then said, 'What do we do with the boy?'

'He's going back to Baltara, apparently,' the first man said.

When the lift reached our floor and the doors opened, the two men got out. Dad leaned forward slightly as he reached for the down arrow. Just before the doors closed, he said, ''Night, gents.'

''Night,' one of them responded, automatically.

Downstairs, Dad grabbed my hand and we sprinted towards Spencer Street Station. We didn't go inside. Instead, Dad pulled me towards the railway lines, lifting me over a fence and racing ahead of me, glancing back every few seconds to make sure I was still following. When I fell and hurt my knee, he helped me up, then grabbed my hand and dragged me on.

For a few minutes, we ran along one of the many tracks that led away from Spencer Street, towards the next station. I watched Dad's thick arms pumping, his feet sure as he navigated the loose stones. Trains on nearby tracks whizzed by, and I wondered whether anybody inside the carriage would spot the man and the boy running through the night, or whether they would be too focused on their own thoughts or their nightly newspaper to notice us.

I wondered how Dad kept doing this. Escaping. Fleeing. And I wondered whether he would ever stop.

# CHAPTER 12

# A GESTURE OF KINDNESS

Dad finally slowed his pace. I'd never realised he could run so fast, or for such a long time. Now, he hunched over, hands on knees, and sucked in several heavy breaths. 'That was a close one, Petey,' he said.

Despite the danger, Dad was giving me a half-grin.

I didn't say anything, just stared at the ground, worrying what was coming next. Dad must have sensed my unease, because he put his arm around me, his deep blue eyes focused on mine. "It'll be okay, son,' he said. 'I promise.'

Dad looked into my eyes searchingly until I gave him a tiny smile of reassurance. Then his voice took on a more enthusiastic tone. 'How about we head off on an adventure? We'll use the money you got us to buy a car and get as far away from here as possible.' As he spoke, it seemed like a plan was forming behind his eyes. 'How does Western Australia sound?'

I wondered what would happen if I just said no, that it was *my* money and I didn't want to go. But I loved being with Dad.

I wouldn't – I couldn't – give that up. No matter how tired or scared I was.

We spent the night in a respite home in the wealthy suburb of Kew, in Melbourne's East. It only opened at 10pm, and provided a small number of homeless people somewhere safe to sleep. Dad and I were the last two people admitted for the night. If I hadn't been with him, I think we would have missed out. As it was, they didn't have a bed for me, so Dad and I had to share.

In the morning, before sunrise, somebody rang a cowbell in the hallway and we left our bedroom, filing after the other men into an old-fashioned dining room with a table too fancy for the men sitting around it. A woman with platinum hair served Dad and I a bowl of soup and a bread roll.

I was staring at the moulded ceiling, with vines and grapes made from plaster, and finishing the last of my soup, when a thin man with greasy slick-backed ginger hair entered the room and clapped his hands for attention.

An ancient man across from me was teering on the edge of sleep, his chin only centimetres from his soup bowl. The sharp clap roused him and he stared at the thin man with watery eyes.

'Time to go,' the thin man said, firmly.

Dad and I walked to Kew Junction, where Dad found a telephone box and closed the door, leaving me outside. As

I waited for him, I watched a group of boys in red and black uniforms emerge from a bakery, laughing and jostling each other while they pulled apart soft rolls. I wondered what it would feel like to be one of them.

None of them saw me. I was glad about that.

Dad made three calls before somebody answered. I heard the deep tone of his voice through the glass wall of the telephone box, but couldn't make out what he was saying. After he hung up, Dad took my hand. He said, 'You look like you could use a treat. How about a milkshake?'

I nodded, and we entered a nearby café. However, once I had been served, Dad told me he'd need to leave me for an hour or so.

I didn't want to stay on my own, especially when the other customers might wonder why I wasn't in school at almost 9am, but I knew better than to protest.

When the waitress stopped at my table, she gave me a gentle smile. She had soft, auburn curls and green eyes. 'Are you dining on your own this morning, young man?' she asked.

'I'm just … um … waiting,' I said, and sucked up the last of my milkshake. 'For my Dad. He won't be long.'

For a moment, concern crossed the waitress's face. Then her smile returned. 'Well, seeing as you're being so patient, how about we get you a warm blueberry muffin?'

My stomach rumbled at the thought of the muffin, but I knew I didn't have any money on me and looked down at the table, my cheeks burning.

'Free of charge, Sweetie,' she said, placing a hand quickly on mine.

Before I had the chance to protest, the waitress was gone. She returned a minute later with a huge muffin. Beaming, I was just about to thank her when I heard the squeal of tyres in the street outside.

Moments later, the café door opened with a harsh jangle and I heard Dad's voice. 'Come on, Petey. We have to go,' he said.

When I saw the look on his face, my stomach tightened. I hesitated momentarily, and he grabbed my arm before steering me away from the table. I glanced back at the muffin, and at the waitress, and realised that I'd never thanked her for her kindness. It was too late now.

Outside, Dad pulled me towards a white valiant with gleaming chrome wheels. It was parked askew, its front bumper almost meeting the curb. I looked up at him and said, 'Wow! Is this ours?'

"It is now," Dad said. His tone made it clear that I shouldn't ask any more questions. Instead, I slid into my seat in silence.

Dad walked around the front of the car, then climbed into the driver's seat, where the keys were waiting for him. He switched on the ignition and the engine roared to life.

Just as we were about to pull away, I heard Dad say, 'What the fuck?'

I looked at Dad, then followed his gaze to see the young waitress running towards us. I wound down my window as quickly as I could.

With a quick move, the waitress thrust a paper bag into my hands. I didn't need to open it to know what it contained. Already, the rich, warm smell of the blueberry muffin had filled the car.

'Thanks,' I managed to say, just before we peeled away from the curb, cutting off traffic amidst a chorus of honking horns.

We drove for ten or fifteen minutes before Dad said, 'We have a long drive ahead of us,' he said. 'Put the radio on if you like.'

I found a station that was playing *Billie Jean* by Michael Jackson, one of my favourite tracks at the time. I didn't know whether Dad would like it, and was surprised when he leaned forward and turned the volume all the way up.

Laughing and singing, we shared the muffin as Dad turned onto the highway and shifted up a couple of gears, putting the city of Melbourne behind us.

\*

For hours, we drove, the bitumen ahead of us seemingly never-ending. It was getting dark when Dad motioned to a neon sign for a 24-hour roadhouse ahead and told me we would rest for a few minutes. He steered the Valiant into a parking spot around the side. I went to the toilet while Dad refuelled and bought us meat pies to take with us. Then we were driving again, the large red sign illuminated against the dark sky in my side mirror. Up ahead, the half-moon made the road glow like a winding river.

For the next four days, we drove. We only stopped for fuel and food and for Dad to sleep for a few hours, always at night. When we entered the Nullarbor Plain, I was amazed to see the red dust that covered the desert floor. In the distance, a caravan of camels slowly made their way across the dry, sandy landscape. The animals stepped in unison, and I wondered where they were headed.

Our second night on the Nullarbor, when it was time for Dad to rest, he pulled off the highway and drove a couple of hundred metres across the dirt so our car wouldn't be visible to the truck drivers who used the road. The day had been hot, and my t-shirt had stuck to me for hours. Now, with the sun having set a couple of hours ago, the air had cooled down, and Dad motioned for me to join him outside the car.

I opened my door and found Dad climbing onto the roof of the Valiant. I did the same. For a while, we lay side by side in silence, looking up at the night sky, which was filled with stars that shone brighter than any I had seen before.

Finally, I said, 'Tell me about one of your jobs, Dad.'

I had suspected, for years, that when he left us in care, Dad was doing something illegal. It was Tina who told me the he robbed banks. I had believed her immediately. It explained a lot.

When Dad spoke, his voice was soft, but it carried perfectly on the still night air. He told me about a job in Bankstown, a suburb of Sydney. He explained that he and his crew had done their homework, and they had pinpointed one security guard as their main obstacle. The guard's name was Clive, a huge man, heavily muscled with a reputation as a real mongrel, the kind of guy who *liked* trouble. It was Dad's job to make sure Clive wouldn't be a problem.

The driver had parked the getaway car away the corner from the busy Bankstown Street. Dad and the other three members of the crew pulled balaclavas over their faces and climbed out of the vehicle, each of them holding a sawn-off shotgun. At precisely 10am, the four of them burst through the front doors of the bank. Two of the three guards immediately put their hands in the air. As they had expected, Clive did not. Instead, as Dad came towards him, he went to draw his gun. He had just unclipped his holster when Dad shoved the two metal barrels of the shotgun against the fleshy folds of the man's throat.

Almost instantly, the big man's demeanour changed. His eyes seem to glaze over, and when Dad told him to get on his fucking knees before he blew his head off, Clive offered no response. Dad told him the same thing, louder this time, but when the guard tried to respond, his words were jumbled. Next, his grey slacks turned black as he pissed himself. Stepping back, appalled, Dad knew Clive was no mongrel. He was a coward. Dad had been prepared to hit him with the stock of his gun, but he could see there was no need. Moments later, Clive lay down voluntarily, staring at the ceiling, muttering incoherently.

When he finished telling the story, Dad was laughing. I made a noise like laughter, but actually I felt sad, thinking about Clive, who was so scared he pissed himself in front of a room full of people he had to work with every day. And sad for Dad, not just because he thought it was funny, but because he seemed incapable of making better choices for himself.

For the first time, I realised how different we were, deep down, and this scared me.

We were about 1000 kilometres from Perth when we made one of our fuel stops. As Dad filled the tank with fuel, he passed me a $2 note and told me to grab myself a cold drink. It was another stinking hot day, and Dad would rarely run the air conditioning in the car because he said it would overheat the engine and use more fuel.

As I entered the roadhouse, an old lady with curly grey hair nodded at me without saying a word. I chose a bottle of Coke from the fridge, paid the lady, and returned to the car where Dad was waiting for me. We had driven just long enough for me to finish my drink when Dad pulled to the side of the road.

'Radiator?' I asked, annoyed that we would have to wait by the side of the road in the heat once again.

'Nope,' Dad replied. 'Time for your first driving lesson.'

A minute later, my heart pounding, I sat in the driver's seat, Dad beside me. He had turned the car off, and instructed me to put my seat belt on, put my foot on the break and turn the key. 'Alright, Petey,' he said. 'This old girl has a 3-on-the-tree gearbox.' I just looked at him blankly, which made him laugh.

Dad seemed to consider giving me a longer explanation, then waved it away and instructed me to put my foot on the clutch and move the stick upwards. 'Good,' he said. 'That's first gear.' He told me to release the clutch slowly, which I did.

The car jumped forward, out of my control suddenly. I panicked and took my foot completely off the clutch. The car jumped forward one more time and came to a stop, the engine stalling.

For a fleeting moment, I felt terror at the thought that I'd damaged the engine, ruining our chances of making it to Perth. Then I heard Dad's laughter. I looked over to see that he was laughing hysterically, tears already beginning to run down his face.

I hadn't seen him laugh like that since I was a little boy.

I finally managed to get the car in 3rd gear and was able to cruise on the correct side of the road. It was after we'd finished the lesson and had returned to our regular seats that he looked at me and said, 'We'll do more of this, Pete. I promise.'

I wanted to believe him.

*

After almost four days on the road, we made it to Perth. We drove past the beautiful Swan River and the expansive Kings Park. It was a well laid out city that looked far less busy than Melbourne, and I found it easier to breathe here, somehow. Dad located an emergency hostel and pulled into a parking space around the back of the building. He was only gone a few minutes before he returned and told me to grab my things.

As we headed inside, Dad said he would contact some friends of his in Port Hedland in the morning and arrange for us to stay with them.

'Are you sure they'll have room for us?' I asked.

'They owe me,' Dad said, removing the room key from his pocket. 'We just need to find a place where we can stay while things calm down. Then we can decide what our next move will be.'

I nodded, pretending to understand what he meant.

The room was simple but clean, with two bunks, one above the other. I chose the top one and climbed up to test it, while Dad lay down on the bed beneath mine with a soft groan. Less than a minute later, I leaned over the edge of the bed to ask Dad what we were going to get for dinner, but he was already asleep.

For a couple of hours, I lay on my bunk, my tummy rumbling, and thought about the people we'd left behind. I knew Tina had a boyfriend and was safe with him and his family. Kelly was living with a foster family and I hoped that they were good to her. We hadn't heard from Dave in months, but I knew he would be alright.

Dave had never visited often. So, when he had, it felt extra special. Somehow, he always seemed to know where to find us. He would show up at some place we were living, unannounced and unaccompanied, usually when Dad was out. We'd ride on his trail bike together, me holding on to his waist. While my sisters and I had been shunted from one form of temporary accommodation to another, Dave had remained with our maternal grandparents, and seemed – by comparison – very lucky. Of course, I had no real idea what Dave had already endured in his young life; it would be many years before I would ask him. I missed him more each time he left.

As I thought about my siblings, I felt a premonitory sense of grief. Despite my dad's insistence to the contrary, I had begun to feel like the chances of us ever living together again were getting ever slimmer.

\*

After spending a couple of days in Perth, we headed off once more, this time for Port Hedland. Dad had explained that it was from this city that minerals and other resources were exported to the rest of the world. I was fascinated to see how busy Port Hedland was despite not having a large population. We made our way through the centre of town and into the suburban streets. Then we pulled into a quiet court and stopped beside a red letterbox with the numbers 47 haphazardly painted in white. The letterbox belonged to a small house with an overgrown lawn. The driveway was littered with car parts and empty beer bottles.

Dad rapped the front door with his thick knuckles, dislodging flakes of white paint. We waited a minute before a guy who looked around twenty-five opened the door. He was tall and very skinny, his arms and chest covered with tattoos. He pushed his sandy blond fringe out of his eyes and squinted slightly at Dad. Then he said, 'Donald?'

'Call me Clarry,' Dad said. 'This is my boy, Pete. You must be Kevin.'

The guy looked from Dad to me and smiled slightly. For the first time, I saw his pockmarked cheeks and the rough orange stubble that covered his chin and jaw. 'G'day, Pete,' he said, extending a long, thin hand. I shook it, quickly, then put my hands in my pockets.

As Dad stepped inside the tiny, fluorescent-lit hallway, Kevin placed a bony hand on my shoulder. He was grinning widely now, his eyes focused intently on mine. 'We're gonna have fun, Pete,' he said. 'Just you wait.'

# CHAPTER 13

# THE SHEEP IN WOLF'S CLOTHING

I walked through the lounge room a couple of steps behind Dad.

In the kitchen, we found another guy who appeared to be a few years younger than Kevin, maybe 19 or 20. He had a young face, but had obviously worked hard to grow a wispy red mustache which ended just below the corners of his mouth. He was sitting at a Formica table surrounded by orange chairs, their vinyl covers spewing foam, intently focused on the task at hand: cutting up what looked like tobacco with a small pair of scissors.

'This is Brett,' Kevin said. 'He doesn't say much, but he's harmless.' As if to demonstrate the validity of his claim, he gave the younger man a hard slap across the top of his shoulders. I winced in sympathy, but Brett didn't even look up from his task. 'Brett, this is Clarry and his son Pete.'

As we passed out of the kitchen and into a wood-paneled hallway beyond, Dad glanced down at me and gave me a lopsided smile. I tried to smile back, but despite my best efforts, my lips refused to cooperate.

Kevin led us down the hall, then opened a door and snapped on the light. 'This is *your* room, boys,' he said, and stepped aside.

Although I'd been mentally preparing myself for disappointment since entering the house, seeing our bedroom still felt sickening. In the middle of the room, there was a double bed, draped with a yellowed bed spread. The room smelled musty and dirty, making my stomach turn. Without looking at me, Dad put a hand on my shoulder, feigning cheerfulness. 'Much appreciated, Kev.'

With the door closed, I sat on the edge of the bed. Dad sat next to me. We said nothing for a while. Then Dad put his hand at the back of my neck and gave it a light squeeze. 'I don't have to tell you not to talk to these boys about what we've been up to, do I?'

I shook my head, and he nodded. Then he said, 'You be polite, but stay away from them.'

I nodded again. When he didn't speak for a minute or so, I asked him something that I had been thinking about since we drove out of Melbourne. 'When will I go to school again?'

Dad pursed his lips, then said, 'Not for a little while, Petey. I'm sorry about that. We need to wait until I've found work at least.' Seeing my disappointment, he squeezed my neck again and said, 'Hey, don't worry. I have a plan.'

After a surprisingly good night's sleep considering the state of our bed, Dad brought me a bowl of cereal. He sat with me while I ate, then told me to get dressed. 'Make sure you look your best,' he said.

I pulled on my dark blue jeans, a light blue t-shirt, and my only pair of shoes: a pair of Dunlop KT26s. I had worn them for the past 12 months but took pride in keeping them clean. Before leaving, I smoothed down my hair with some water. Then we set out across a large, vacant lot behind our house. It was the length of several football fields, and barren except for the occasional scrubby tree or the rusted carcass of an abandoned car.

Fifteen minutes later, we stepped into the refreshingly air conditioned interior of the local Kmart. Dad looked down at me and winked. I knew what that meant: keep your mouth shut. My stomach began to churn, and I told myself to relax, reminding myself that he had a plan.

Dad sauntered up to the information desk, where a woman with platinum curls and bright pink nails gave him a broad smile. Flexing his muscular arms across his chest, he asked to see the manager, using the tone he always reserved for women. She asked whether the manager was expecting us. Dad said, "No, he isn't, but I promise ya, love, we'll only take a few minutes of his time.'

For a moment, the woman hesitated. Then Dad smiled more broadly and she got up from her seat, revealing a large bottom covered by a tight black skirt. I felt my cheeks redden and looked at Dad. He was watching the woman walk away appreciatively.

While we waited, we sat on a couple of hard plastic chairs in sight of the information desk. After returning to the desk, the platinum-haired woman looked up and gave us each a smile, one of reassurance to me, and a more coy one for my father. Finally, a man in his thirties emerged from an office somewhere beyond the information desk and walked towards us. He wore a long-sleeved shirt with a bright red tie. His hair was slicked back.

We stood up and my dad held out a hand, which the man shook firmly.

'I'm Warren,' the man said, with a practiced smile. 'What can I do for you today?'

'G'day, Warren,' Dad began, then shifted his tone subtly. 'I'm Clarence Reynolds. This is my son, Peter.'

Great, I thought. Another surname to remember.

I shook the man's hand.

'Nice to meet you, Peter,' Warren said.

'Anyway, Peter here's just turned fifteen,' Dad continued. 'He finished year 10 back East and he's looking for a full-time job.'

Now, Warren looked at me with greater attention, clearly sizing me up. I was tall for my age, but I was doubtful this man would believe my dad's claim. My palms began to sweat and I had to force my breathing to remain steady.

Warren's eyes met mine and narrowed, and for a moment, I was sure he would challenge me to prove my age. Then he nodded, and addressed me directly, saying, 'Peter, when can you start?'

In his office, Warren took down my details, many of which my dad made up on the spot. While he jotted down the answers he required, he told us about a former employee who had just left, after shoplifting almost 900 dollars' worth of goods. I didn't look at Dad when I heard this. In fact, I looked down at my feet. But I could hear Dad making the right sort of noises, and Warren seemed convinced by his performance.

Warren was the sort of guy my dad would often make fun of. A mug. Too trusting. But to his face, Dad was nothing but polite.

Warren seemed ready to confirm my hire when he asked Dad for my birth certificate. Now I looked up, my cheeks burning.

Dad didn't hesitate. 'No problem at all,' he said. 'We haven't unpacked our belongings yet, but as soon as we do, I'll get Peter to bring the certificate to work with him.'

For a moment, Warren hesitated, his smile dimming slightly. Then it was back, his arm outstretched, and he was shaking both of our hands. 'Well, Peter,' he said, as we left his office, 'We are delighted to have you here.'

*

My first shift was the following Monday. I arrived at 8am for my scheduled 8:30am start. I was dressed in the navy-blue polo top that Kmart supplied and Dad and I had managed to scrape enough money together to buy some black slacks and dress shoes. After a quick induction, consisting of a tour of the 'floor' and the lunchroom and an explanation of the pay cycle, I was put to work. My first task was to help another staff member in the stationary section. I found the work enjoyable – almost fun – solving problems for people, helping them find what they needed and unpacking pallets of stock as they arrived in the warehouse.

The following Monday, following my shift, I collected my pay from the paymaster, who sat behind a small window near the lunchroom. I was excited. I had worked hard all week and eagerly signed Peter Reynolds where he indicated. He handed me a small yellow envelope. Outside, I checked it and discovered $85. I slipped the envelope into the pocket of my slacks, and kept my hand against it all the way home.

Ten minutes later, I walked through the front door and down the hallway to our bedroom, where Dad was lying on the bed reading the newspaper. I pulled the envelope out of my pocket and presented it to him. My heart swelled at the look of pride in his eyes as he examined the money.

'You know how much I appreciate this, Petey, don't you?' Dad asked, with a stare that told me he meant it. I could only nod. Then he stood up, slipped the envelope into the back pocket of his jeans, and put his arm around me, saying, 'I think you deserve a counter meal. We both do.'

We quickly fell into our new routine. I got up every morning looking forward to working, and walked across the grassy stretch behind our house while Dad and the others were asleep. I worked for a few hours, then had a sandwich I'd made at home while sitting in the lunchroom alone. That was, except for Fridays, when I was allowed to spend some money from my pay at Holly's Café in-store. I always ordered the same thing: a chicken and cheese toasted sandwich with a side of Holly's famous chips and gravy.

There were plenty of teenagers working at the store, but I didn't spend much time with them. To me, they seemed lazy, more interested in mucking around and flirting than dealing with customers. I always took pride in my work and quickly became known as the kid who could unpack a pallet load of stock twice as fast as even veteran team members. I was also the first person to try and help customers.

I had been in my position almost two months when I heard my name being called through the store speaker system. This was a first, and I half-walked, half-ran, towards Warren's office, my mind racing. Had they found out about my Dad? About me? If so, I knew that everything was about to come crashing down.

I knocked tentatively on Warren's door. It was only a few seconds before he swung the door open, greeting me with a quick, 'Come in, Peter.' Standing up, he perched on the edge of his desk and said, 'I'm sure you know we've been watching you.'

My face must have registered my shock, because he immediately looked apologetic. 'You're not in any trouble.'

'Oh,' I said. 'Good.' But I still wouldn't allow myself to relax. Not until I knew exactly what he wanted.

Warren said, 'It's your feedback forms. I wanted to talk to you about them.'

He opened a manilla folder and removed ten or more small white forms with handwriting on them. I had seen customers filling them out occasionally and placing them into little boxes on their way out of the store.

Warren shook his head. Then, he smiled. 'These are incredible,' he said. 'Glowing. I've simply never seen feedback this positive, not even when *I* was working the floor.' Suddenly, I felt a wave of relief. I tried to say something, but no words came out. 'Because of that, I would like to formally offer you a position as the manager of the furniture section," Waren said. 'We … ah … wouldn't usually offer this sort of position to a fifteen-year-old, but I feel confident you can handle the responsibility. How would you feel about that? Of course, there would be a significant pay rise.'

For a few moments, I stared at him, stunned. Then I beamed and stuck my hand out. 'I'd love that,' I said. 'Thank you. Thanks. Very much. I … wow.'

As he shook my hand, Warren laughed. 'That's great to hear.'

That day, I ran all the way across the grassy stretch, making it home in less than five minutes, ignoring the sweat that poured down my face and sides. I passed Kevin and Brett, who were playing cards in the kitchen, the room filled with cigarette smoke.

In our room, I said, 'Dad, you are not going to believe this …' and proceeded to tell him exactly what had happened in Warren's office earlier that day.

As I talked, Dad shook his head slowly, a tiny smile playing on his lips. Then, when I finished, he kissed me on the forehead before holding me at arm's length. 'That's amazing, Petey,' he said.

'And it means more pay,' I said, knowing that the question must be bubbling just below the surface for him and preferring to bring it up myself rather than hearing him ask it out loud. 'At least 30 dollars more per week.'

'See?' Dad said, ruffling my hair. 'Did I come up with a plan, or what?'

*

During my first few weeks as Manager, I learned how to control the inventory for my department and continued to just work hard and say no more than I had to, which was something my team seemed to appreciate. Despite my age – the age they assumed I was, anyway – nobody had treated me with anything but respect. In fact, due to a couple of key staff being dismissed for reasons I never discovered, I had been handed the management of another two departments. This meant that, before my twelfth birthday, I was running the Furniture, Floor Coverings and Tools departments.

In my attempts to avoid awkward questions from my team members, I spent most of my free time talking to the cleaning staff. I hit it off with a girl named Jacinta, who had begun working at the store on the recommendation of her aunt. She had dark hair and eyes, an upturned nose, and was strikingly pretty, even in her cleaning uniform. We ate lunch together sitting in the loading bay and sharing whatever we'd brought from home that day. That was except Fridays, when we would eat at Holly's.

It was during one of our lunches at Holly's that Jacinta asked whether I would like to come to a party with her on the weekend.

I wanted desperately to go, but knew that it wasn't right. After all, I was five years younger than she was. It hurt to see the look of disappointment in her eyes when I said no, even more so because I couldn't offer her an explanation.

The following Monday, after collecting my pay, I walked to the newsagent to buy comics. When I left the store, I was holding an *Archie and Jughead,* an *Incredible Hulk,* and *The Amazing Spiderman*. I was so excited to read my spiderman comic that I didn't even wait to get home; I began reading while walking across the messy scrubland on the way to our house.

I had been walking for a minute or so when I became aware of a soft footstep behind me and turned my head. I was relieved to see Kevin's lanky form, and stopped, waiting for him to catch up. He was smoking a cigarette, and jogged slightly as he approached. He had come to see me at work occasionally and had been waiting when I left work a few times. The first time, he had explained that Port Hedland could be a pretty rough place and that he wanted to make sure I got home safe. We were both AFL fans, so we usually passed the time talking about the latest results.

Today, Kevin's normally relaxed expression was gone. He smiled – more of a grin, really – but he didn't seem happy, exactly. 'Watcha reading?' he asked.

'Spidey,' I said.

'Oh, yeah? Who's he fighting this week?'

'Doc Ock,' I said.

He didn't seem to be listening. 'Your Dad asked me to walk you home,' he said.

'Oh,' I said, a little surprised. 'Okay.'

He pulled his cigarettes out of his shirt pocket, then stopped to light one. With it lit, he took it out of his mouth and offered it to me. I shook my head, and he slipped it between his lips once more before taking a long drag. 'You like living here?' he asked.

'It's okay, I guess,' I said.

'You do it with that girl yet? The cleaning chick?'

I knew what he meant. I didn't like hearing him talk about Jacinta like that. I shook my head. 'We're just friends.'

He nodded. 'Well, don't wait. *She's* not gonna. They never do.'

We began walking again. Although he was taller than me, Kevin slouched, so when I glanced to my left his eyes met mine.

'What do you think she's gonna say?' Kevin asked, his tone flat, 'When she finds out you're a virgin?'

I sensed, rather than saw, his hand reach for me, but I wasn't quick enough to avoid his grasp. Suddenly, he was holding my shoulder, turning me to face him.

'What–?' I asked. 'What do you want?'

But I knew. And he knew that I knew.

As Kevin reached for me with his other hand, I threw the comics at him. It was just enough of a distraction for me to break his grasp. Then I was running through the scrub and the red dirt, like I had run in that race so long ago.

I didn't turn to see whether he was following. I knew there was no way he could catch me.

When I got home, I ran to mine and Dad's room. Dad wasn't there, so I pushed the tiny chest of drawers we shared up against the door, then put my back against it. After I had been sitting there for a few minutes, I heard a soft knock at the door and Kevin spoke. 'Hey, Pete, are you in there, mate?'

I didn't say anything.

I heard the door handle turn, and felt a little pressure against my back as he tried to open the door.

'Hey. You know I was just kidding, right?'

Again, I said nothing. Then I heard Kevin swear under his breath and the thud of his fist or foot striking the door.

I sat like that until I heard the front door open and Dad's familiar footsteps crossed the linoleum of the kitchen. When I heard him offering a muffled hello to Brett, then Kevin, I stood up and pushed the chest of drawers back against the wall, then sat on the edge of the bed.

When he came into the bedroom, Dad seemed to sense that something was wrong, but he didn't ask me outright. I told him that work had been good, and handed him my pay.

Dad said he'd bought a roast chicken, and asked whether I wanted a sandwich. I said I did, but that I'd like to eat it in our bedroom.

It was only hours later, when the lights were out and Dad was lying in the bunk beneath mine, that I told him what Kevin had tried to do. At first, I thought he might be angry at me – I'm not sure why – but of course he wasn't. He stood up and kissed my forehead, then said, 'It's alright, Petey. Get some sleep now.'

Despite his words, I lay awake for a long time, until I heard my Dad's rhythmic breathing. Then I, too, fell asleep.

I had no idea what time it was when I was woken by the sound of yelling from somewhere beyond our door. I sat up and there was the sound of a heavy blow and something wooden splintering.

I stumbled out of our bedroom, rubbing my eyes, to find Brett lying across a broken coffee table and Kevin face-down on the carpet, his nose shattered.

'Get in the car, Petey,' Dad said, his fists clenched and bloody. I did as he commanded. Minutes later, he emerged from the house, tossed our bags across the back seat, and threw the car into reverse.

For the next few days, we lived in emergency accommodation a few kilometres from the centre of town. Each morning, my dad drove me to work, and was there to pick me up when I emerged from the building each afternoon. Occasionally, I looked in the direction of Kevin's place – I couldn't help it – but I never saw him or anybody else emerge from it.

It was Friday, and I was looking forward to meeting Jacinta at Holly's Café for lunch, when I heard my name called over the intercom once more.

I walked to Warren's office without the fear I had felt at this sort of summons months ago. Warren and I had met regularly since then, and he had never been anything except complimentary of my work and conduct.

This time, however, it wasn't just Warren waiting for me. There were two other men flanking his desk. Both wore suits.

Warren wasn't looking at me; he was staring at his desk.

One of the men who spoke. 'Peter Norris?' he asked. He didn't wait for me to respond before adding, 'We've just taken your father into custody. He told us where to find you.'

I wondered whether it was Kevin or Brett who'd dobbed Dad in, not that it really mattered.

As Warren looked up at me, my heart sank. I expected him to be angry, to yell at me, but when he walked around his desk and looked down at me, he simply held out his hand. I thought of the first day I had met him; the way he had hired me on the spot with little more than a handshake.

I shook Warren's hand again and felt my eyes begin to sting with tears. I swallowed hard and said, 'I'm sorry I disappointed you.'

'Peter,' Warren said, 'These men tell me you're only eleven years old.' He waited for me to look at him, then added, 'I'm only disappointed that we have to say goodbye today.'

The two officers had put me in the back of the car when I heard Warren calling my name and turned to see the manager jogging towards the police car. With the officers' permission, he handed me an envelope that he explained was my final pay. 'He earned it,' Warren said.

As we drove away, I turned to see Warren standing in the parking lot as other staff members emerged from the store, Jacinta included. A part of me was glad I didn't ever have to tell them the truth about my age. It saved me from having to witness the shock and embarrassment on their faces.

As we drove out of town, one of the officers told me that Dad was being transported to Perth and that I would be told more at the 'home'.

That night, after being shown into a room I would have to share with three other boys, I lay in bed long after lights out.

Finally, I got up and made my way to the bathroom, the only place where I could be alone.

There, I opened the yellow envelope, and found an extra two weeks' pay along with a handwritten note. It read:

Peter, keep dreaming and being exactly who you are. We all believe in you. One day, when you're ready, you will be a remarkable leader. In the meantime, you've given us an incredible story to tell. – W.

My back against the bathroom door, I allowed myself to cry, my sobs reverberating off the tiled walls.

# CHAPTER 14

# MAKING MY OWN LUCK

After my first night in the respite home in Perth, I was told I would be allowed to see Dad in the remand centre before he was taken back to Fremantle Prison. I was accompanied to a reception room in the remand centre by a burly guard and was told that I wasn't allowed to touch my father.

Sitting across a white plastic table from me, Dad looked haggard. I asked him when would he get out, when could we live together again. Dad could only shrug.

Our visit was over too soon.

As I rode in the back seat of a nondescript car on my way back to the respite home, I squeezed my fists until my nails left red crescents in my palms. Why couldn't we just live in peace and enjoy a normal life as a family?

I felt physically sick as I walked back through the glass doors of the respite home. The night before, one of the older boys had flicked my ear as he walked past, and I had considered punching him in the jaw, but I knew that that would only mean punishment.

My experience at Kmart had proved to me that I could support myself, while living at Baltara showed me that not everybody in a position of authority could be trusted. If I was going to get out of here, I couldn't wait for somebody to do it for me.

The next morning, I got up at 7am, showered and ate a quick breakfast of toast and vegemite. I had already packed my bag, giving Tom the Turtle pride of place atop my meagre belongings. When I had arrived at the place, the centre's manager had insisted that this was not a prison. We would be largely left to our own recognisance. I hadn't known exactly what that meant, but, as I walked out, nobody tried to stop me. Nobody seemed to care.

I walked down streets already beginning to bake. I wasn't sure where I was going. I just wanted to be alone.

I wandered the streets of the city for the day, long after my feet grew hot through the soles of my shoes and I could feel the bite of blisters on my ankles. I stopped occasionally, to sit under the shade of a tree or to drink from a public drinking fountain. I hadn't brought anything to eat and, as the sun began to set, my stomach grumbled. An hour later, still without eating anything, I curled up on a park bench in Kings Park.

Over the next few days, I came to realise there was a community of kids who lived like I did, roaming the streets during the day and finding places to sleep at night. It was from them that I learned how to survive. Milk and bread were usually delivered in the early hours of the morning, before the sun rose too high, and were left at the front or back door of cafés and restaurants. These were easy pickings. When I told one of the kids – a boy named Colin, who looked fourteen or fifteen and walked with a limp – that I had been cold during the night, he took me on what he called an 'excursion' to find more suitable clothing. We found several layers, including a thick fleece, on a backyard clothesline. While Colin coached me from the safety of the laneway, I scrambled up the old wooden fence before dropping noiselessly into the garden, creeping up to the clothesline, and snatching the clothing in mere seconds.

I was good at this.

The streets could be harsh. There were no free passes regardless of how young you were. Some of the boys formed small gangs to support and protect each other, and were only too happy to start a fight to show how tough they were. At first, Colin and I tried to keep out of sight of the bigger, rougher boys, but this couldn't last forever. One morning, I woke to find one of these boys raiding my bag. Without a word, I pushed myself up onto my knees and delivered a punch to his nose that squashed it flat.

From that point on, I refused to take a backward step. I copped my fair share of beatings, often by boys much older and bigger than me, but as time went on, I became tougher. It was during this time that Colin chose to go his own way. Maybe he thought I'd end up seriously injured … or worse. He always was good at self-preservation.

Sometimes, my running prowess came to the rescue. This allowed me to escape larger gangs, homeowners who weren't satisfied with merely shouting at me as I snatched their belongings out of backyards and off front stoops, and even the police.

After a couple of months, I found a larger group to hang out with. This meant that I had to give up some of my independence, but I liked knowing that I would get to see the same faces when I returned to our hangout – a condemned factory – in the evenings. If any of us came across any money during the day, it was understood that he or she would ensure each person was fed and provided with essentials. Even then, I was impressed with the way that these kids, without adult intervention, had managed to create a culture where each person was looked after by the community.

My best friend at the factory was Mark. He was two years older than me, tall and very strong. Like me, he had tight curly hair, except his was blonde and longer than mine. His eyes were dark brown, and he had a cheeky grin and a laugh that made everyone around him giggle. On several occasions Mark saved me, and the other kids, from a certain beating, either by talking his way out of it, or – when necessary – by fighting. Mark's father was also in jail, but his mother had formed a nasty drug habit and was no longer capable of taking care of him. He had left before social services had a chance to intervene. By the time I met him, he had been on the streets for three years.

For a few weeks after arriving at the factory, I barely left Mark's side. It felt like what I imagined it would be to have a protective big brother. We would often share a blanket or the clothes we were able to steal. Sometimes, lying next to him, I thought about my real brother and wondered how he was doing.

The last time I'd seen Dave was when we were living in Bagdally and Dad was working as a cleaner at our primary school. Dave hadn't visited often, but a few times, always when Dad was out, he had shown up on his trail bike and asked whether I'd like to go for a ride. For a couple of hours, we would ride together, my arms wrapped around his waist as he drove around the Northern suburbs of city. I admired the way he never seemed to need anybody's permission to do what he wanted. I envied his ability to live freely, seemingly without a worry in the world. After our rides, he drove me back to our commission house and gave me a casual wave. Then he was gone, always too quickly, and I was left to miss him desperately, never knowing how long it would be until I saw him again.

I was dreaming of Dave when Mark shook me awake gently. I opened my eyes and saw how dark the factory was. I sat up.

'Everything okay?' I asked.

Mark nodded, then pointed to my shoes, indicating that I should put them on. 'I need to show you something.'

We made our way along backstreets and down alleyways that I had come to know well. Mark didn't say a word until we reached a warehouse surrounded by a high, chain-link fence. Mark said, 'I've had my eye on this place for a while. I always thought there was something suss about it. Apparently, Naomi saw a bunch of guys here this afternoon, unloading something heavy. I figure it's worth a look.'

I could see why Mark was interested. The warehouse looked dilapidated, but the padlock on the back fence was shiny. Side by side, we climbed the fence and sat atop it only a moment before dropping onto the tarmac below.

We ran across an empty lot and stopped beneath a window that was lit from within. I could hear men talking and laughing. I didn't recognise the language they spoke, but thought it sounded Italian or Greek. Standing up slowly, Mark looked through the window, then whistled softly through his teeth. I stood on my tiptoes to peer inside.

The warehouse was made up of two rooms. There was a large room in front of us, where six men sat around a table playing cards. In the room beyond, I saw a van and, beside it, what appeared at first to be a large crate the size of a small washing machine. As my eyes adjusted to the gloom inside the building, however, I could see that it wasn't a crate: it was a safe. It had been broken open, and there were several bags of what I would only assume were money exposed within, along with a smattering of coins that glinted in the overhead lights.

Further along the exterior wall, we discovered a door that led straight into the smaller room. To our shock, it was unlocked. Slipping off our shoes, we sidled through the open door and into the room. Blood thudded in my ears and I felt much like I had the first time my sisters and I had entered the high school in search of our first 'score'.

As we got closer to the safe, the men's conversation grew louder. The air was thick with smoke from their cigarettes and cigars, and I willed myself not to cough.

When we reached the large black safe, I hid behind it, staying out of view of the men at the table. Mark, I noticed, had hung back a few metres, a good idea since there was no way the safe's door could hide his bulky frame.

Reaching into one of the sacks in the safe, I confirmed that it was filled with money. Each bundle of cash was folded and secured with a red elastic band. Telling myself not to be greedy – that, if we only took a little bit of the money, the men might not notice – I slipped the single wad into my pocket. I was about to crawl away from the safe when I saw Mark motioning to a bag on the ground, the source of the coins I had spotted through the window.

The bag of coins was much heavier than I'd expected. I had to strain to pick it up and almost dropped it. Adjusting it in my arms, I began to crawl away from the safe, sweat running down my forehead.

We were almost at the door when I saw a long table, on which six handguns had been placed. Immediately, I realised that these guys – whoever they were – were serious criminals. For a moment, Mark seemed as if he might be about to take one of weapons, but I put my body between him and the table and we both made it through the door and into the lot without incident.

Moments later, Mark climbed over the fence, then motioned for me to toss the bag of coins. I wasn't sure that I'd be able to do it, but I guess the adrenaline had kicked in, because I tossed them high and watched them sail over the chain link before Mark caught the bag, only spilling a few onto the cobblestones.

When we were a couple of blocks away from the warehouse, we both slumped against a wall, giggling with relief. Mark put his arm around my shoulders and said, 'Holy shit, Pete. You've got balls of steel!'

I just laughed and tried not to show how relieved I was to be out of that room and away from those men.

A few minutes later, we sat down at a bus stop, and I pulled the banknotes out of my pocket and started counting. We'd scored exactly $650 in cash, and who knows how much more in coins.

When we got back to the factory, it was just before midnight, but we didn't care. Mark and I stood on a long table and Mark yelled, 'Everyone up!'

Moments later, kids began to emerge from darkened pockets of the building. There were at least fifteen of them. When they were gathered, Mark said, 'Who wants Maccas? Our shout!'

The nearest McDonald's was only a few blocks away. We were all used to walking past it, staring longingly at the diners within. Now, we poured through the entrance, taking up four booths.

I could see that the young girl behind the counter was nervous, so I approached with money in hand, and announced, 'We'll take 50 cheeseburgers, 30 large fries, 15 large cokes and 30 boxes of cookies.' When she hesitated, I said, 'Please.' I took the red elastic band off the wad of cash and slapped the money on the countertop. 'Just take it out of that.' Behind me, my friends cheered as the cashier relayed the order to those in the kitchen.

As I ate my burger and fries and listened to the other kids chattering and laughing around me, I thought about the cash we'd taken. The guys we had stolen it from had clearly stolen it, so I knew I shouldn't feel too guilty. But I still did. I thought about the guns, and the way Mark had wanted to grab one, and I knew that, if I kept going like this, it wouldn't be long before I ended up like my father.

I thought about my dad, and our adventures crossing the Nullarbor Plain. It all seemed so long ago now. I longed to be with him and Tina and Kelly and Dave, somewhere we would be safe. In this fantasy, I even imagined my mum was there, but I couldn't see her face any more; she was merely a presence, warm and reassuring.

I tried to eat my cookies, but I could hardly taste them, so put them in my pocket for later. I was almost glad when the girl from behind the counter told us it was time to leave and we returned to the warehouse.

The following day, while Mark and the other kids headed to a local arcade to check out a new swashbuckling game called *Dragon's Lair*, I returned to the warehouse alone. I packed a bag and got onto the first bus to the city's centre, then walked to the remand centre where I had last seen my dad.

I swung open the large glass door and entered the building. Immediately, the hairs on the back of my neck stood up and I had to force myself to approach the front desk. Behind a glass window sat a large, middle-aged men with a thick greying moustache stained yellow from years of smoking. He lowered his thick glasses and regarded me with dark, empty eyes. 'What do you want?' he asked.

'I'm here to see my dad,' I said, suddenly aware of the grime on my clothes and my messy hair. 'His name's Clarence Norris.'

'Who brought you here, young man?'

'I – I came on my own,' I said.

The man looked me up and down. Then his features softened and he said, 'Follow me.'

I followed the guard down a long hallway. Then he pulled out a large set of keys and unlocked a heavy metal door. He motioned for me to enter the room, then instructed me to take a seat at the table. It was the same room where I'd last seen my dad.

I sat down and waited. I glanced at the large glass window along one wall, recalling movies and TV shows where people would watch the prisoners from behind mirrors like this one while remaining hidden from sight. It made me think of the people who had always seemed to be waiting just beyond my view, watching me and my family. Often, they said they were there to help. But they never were. Not really.

I hoped nobody was watching me now.

After a few minutes, I heard the door open and the same guard entered. This time he was smiling. 'Look who I found,' he said.

The next person to walk through the door was my dad. He clearly hadn't been told who had come to visit, because he looked both shocked and pleased as I leapt up from my chair, sending it flying.

'Petey!' Dad said, his voice cracking. He wrapped his arms around me and I felt his chest heave as he sobbed. Finally, pulling back so that he could see me, he stroked my hair. I saw the tears in his eyes as he said, 'Where did they put you?'

I ignored his question and buried my face in his chest, feeling tears streaming down my face. This was home to me, with or without a roof over my head. We didn't speak for a few minutes, both of lost in the peace of each other's embrace. Then, finally, my dad stepped back and steered me back to the table. I picked up my chair and sat down opposite him.

Now, my dad repeated his question, his expression one of concern.

'I'm in a really nice place, Dad,' I lied. 'Don't worry about it.'

Dad nodded. Whether he believed me, I couldn't tell.

We spent the next thirty minutes talking, his hand stroking mine over the tabletop. He told me that his case was going well. He had found a public defender who was a real pitbull, apparently.

Too soon, the guard opened the door and said, 'Time to go, I'm afraid.'

'Thanks, Gary,' Dad said, standing up. Before he left, he raised my chin and looked into my eyes. 'Wherever you are, Petey, I need you to know I will find you.' Tears rolled down his cheeks.

'I know, Dad,' I said. 'I know.'

Dad kissed my forehead and left the room, Gary a couple of steps behind him. The door closed behind them.

As I waited for Gary to return, I cried again, harder this time, my head on my arms, thinking about my dad's words. 'I will find you,' he had said. He could do it; I knew that. He had done it before. I just had to be patient. And I needed somewhere else to stay in the meantime. Somewhere closer to the rest of my family.

By the time Gary returned to walk me out, I knew what I had to do.

# CHAPTER 15

# FOLLOWING DAD'S PATH

The first car I hitched a ride in took me less than 100kms from Perth, but I didn't complain. I was just happy that the driver hadn't seemed too concerned to find a young boy travelling on his own.

The man's name was Barry. I guessed he was in his mid-fifties. He was extremely talkative, so for the hour we rode together, I hardly got a word in. Barry said that he was a mechanic and worked in a small garage south of Perth. Apparently, he'd been visiting his mother, whose health was failing.

When he asked me where I was headed, I considered lying, but said, 'Shepparton.' He seemed not to know where Shepparton was, so I added, 'Victoria.'

Barry shook his head. 'You're a brave kid,' he said. 'Travelling thousands of K's across the Nullarboor on your own. I've never even been to Victoria.' For a moment, his mood darkened slightly at this realisation; then he shook it off and said, 'How old are ya?'

'I'm eleven,' I replied, automatically, then laughed as I realised something myself. 'Actually, I'm twelve. Today's my birthday.'

'Well, happy birthday, mate,' Barry said, shaking my hand.

Finally, he said, 'Well, this is where I turn off.'

I saw that we had reached a crossroad and nodded.

'If you like, I could grab you something from the café before I go.' Barry pointed to a small, white-brick building.

I nodded gratefully, realising for the first time how hungry I was.

Inside, Barry told me I could order anything I liked. I asked the waitress for a hamburger with the lot and a chocolate milkshake. When she asked Barry what he would like, he glanced down at me, confessing, 'I'm meant to be on a diet.' But after only a moment's hesitation, he told the waitress that he would have the same.

We ate in a comfortable silence for at least twenty minutes. I was just finishing up when Barry told me he had to go to the toilet. Upon his return, Barry presented me with a small shopping bag's worth of fresh baked goods. I was about to protest, but he cut me off, saying, 'Wouldn't want to see you go off hungry.' Then he smiled and held out his meaty right hand, ready for me to shake it once more. Instead, I stepped forward and wrapped my arms around him, my face momentarily pressed against his generous belly.

'Thank you,' I said.

When I stepped back, I saw the emotion in his eyes. I knew that he wanted to make sure I would be okay, so I gave him what I hoped looked like a confident smile. A moment later, with a nod of his head and only a brief glance back at me through the front window, Barry left. As I watched his car pull away from the curb and felt the weight of the bag in my fingers, I thought that it was nice to be reminded that there were decent people in the world.

As it turned out, I would meet a few of them while hitchhiking. Very few people ever inquired about my age or why I was travelling on my own. Maybe they were just grateful for the company. When people did ask, I told the truth. And I made sure they knew I was thankful for any help they gave me.

I took every opportunity I could to nap. Sometimes, I dreamt about Dad. We were getting further apart with every hour that passed, but I told myself that one day I would look up and find him standing there, his hand out, waiting to take me away once more.

After several trips and countless conversations, I reached the small town of Eucla, almost 1500 kilometres from Perth. This was one of the smallest towns I'd ever seen, without even a welcome sign. I was about to head towards the pub in search of my next ride when a car beeped me from behind and I turned around to see a police cruiser approaching.

Maybe they'd been tipped off by another traveller. I don't know. But they seemed to be waiting for me. They asked me why I was hitchhiking through town. I lied, telling them that I'd come to see my grandmother. This didn't work, because – with only 50 residents – the cops knew everybody. Then they asked who they could call on my behalf, and I gave them the only person whose name and number I still knew: my caseworker's.

At the police station, which was located in a small air-conditioned building, one of the officers telephoned the number I had given her, while the other got me a cup of tea. I drank it slowly, while eating the last of the pastries that Barry had bought for me.

It was decided that, after spending a night at the station, I would be put on a bus back to Perth. I hated the thought of going back the way I had come, but I knew that trying to escape would be futile.

*

When I stepped off the bus the next evening, I expected my caseworker to be angry, or at least disappointed. Instead, she told me that she had spoken to my sister Tina, who had agreed that I could live with her. Amazingly, Tina had even been granted temporary custody of me. I never found out exactly what went on behind the scenes to make that happen, but I suspect that somebody realised I wasn't going to stop running until I was back on the East Coast.

The next day, I eagerly climbed onto a train bound for Adelaide; it would be there that I would catch another train to Melbourne. For some reason, I had been given an entire sleeping cabin, and I took the opportunity to spread out; that is, when I wasn't exploring the rest of the train or chatting to the other passengers.

When we arrived in Melbourne, I was met by another government caseworker. I had stopped trying to remember their names. She drove me back to Shepparton, a relatively boring drive up the Hume Highway. We didn't talk much.

As we entered Shepparton, I felt butterflies in my stomach. It had been some time since I had seen my sister and wasn't sure what to expect. We pulled into a block of units and drove to the one at the far end. It had a small, unkempt garden under the front window and a large number 7 in the centre of the door.

As I climbed out of the car, the front door of the house flew open and Tina ran down the path. I barely had time to take in her new blond curls before her arms were wrapped around me, her body warm against mine. Then she held me at arm's length, examining my face while I examined hers. I was shocked at how much older and more mature she seemed than the last time I saw her. 'Hey, Pete,' she said softly.

'Hey, Teens,' I said.

That evening, while we ate dinner, Tina told me what she had been up to since I'd last seen her. She had met a man named Bedri and they had fallen in love. She had wanted to marry him, but at only 16, with Bedri already in his early twenties, she had to apply for permission from the State. After several months, her application had been approved, and they had been married at the local Registry Office in Melbourne.

As Tina spoke, Bedri sat beside her. He had a quiet energy and kind eyes. I knew instinctively that Tina had made a good choice this time.

The week after I arrived at her house, Tina took me to Shepparton High School, where I enrolled in Year 7 despite having missed much of the previous year's schooling. On my first day, I realised just how big a hindrance that missed schooling would be. In Maths, without the basic foundational knowledge, I struggled to understand what the teacher was saying, and found my mind wandering. I was a little better in English. At lunchtime, I couldn't muster the energy to make new friends, so I found a quiet spot behind one of the portables where I could eat lunch on my own. I wondered what Dad was doing right now.

After that first day, I decided I wasn't going back. Each morning, Tina would send me off to school, waving goodbye from her front door. I would say goodbye and head off in the direction of school, then turn up a quiet street and wait at the local playground until I knew Tina and Bedri would have left for the day. Then I would retrace my steps and let myself back into the house.

I had been doing this for a week when I realised that I was missing an opportunity by just hanging around watching daytime TV and waiting for Tina to return. The next morning, I walked a few blocks away from Tina's unit, then knocked on the door of a random house.

No answer.

I walked around the side of the house, and was just about to open the side gate, which I could already see was unlocked, when I heard the front door open behind me.

'Hello?' somebody called out. A woman's voice.

I walked back to the front of the house. For a moment, I almost panicked, fearing that she would call the police. Then I saw her expression – the way she held her terry-towel robe at the neck – and I relaxed. 'I'm sorry to bother you,' I said. 'Is Tom here? He asked me to come and meet him this morning.'

'Tom?' The woman looked confused now.

'Yes,' I said. 'Tom Perry. He lives here, doesn't he?'

'No,' the woman answered. 'I'm sorry. He doesn't.'

Shaking my head, I said, 'I must have gotten the address wrong.' Then, apologising profusely, I walked away. She gave me a friendly wave just before stepping back inside and closing the front door.

A block away, I chose another house and repeated the process. This time, when I was sure nobody was home, I let myself into the backyard. I tried prising open each window until I found one that had been left unlocked. Slipping it open with a deft movement, I hoisted myself up onto the windowsill and shimmied inside.

Half an hour later, I had filled my backpack with a range of items, including jewellery and cash. I left the way I came and closed the window behind me.

Nobody saw me leave.

This quickly became my daily routine. Whenever a home-owner was inside, I would pretend I had the wrong address. Nobody ever challenged me on it. Sometimes, despite my best efforts, I couldn't gain access to a property without breaking a window, something I didn't want to do because I figured it might be loud enough to attract unwanted attention and because there was something about seeing the broken glass that made the act of stealing feel worse somehow. This wasn't the only thing that made me feel guilty. I hated stealing from a child's room, breaking open their piggy bank or taking notes saved in a special box. But, at these moments, I would remind myself that, when Dad came back for me, every dollar I had would give us more time together.

It was my Dad who had told me to always have an exit plan. I had recalled this advice plenty of times and was in the habit of planning for contingencies. That was, until I saw the house with the new paintjob and immaculate hedging. I knew that they would have some good stuff inside.

I knocked and, after receiving no answer, made my way down the side of the house, where the hedge continued, shielding me from view of any neighbours. I tried the back door. As I had expected, it was locked. Next to the door was a louvre window. This meant that, to gain access, I couldn't simply lift a window up to squeeze through, as I had done so many times before. Instead, I would have to be more inventive.

Looking around the garden for a rock, I gave one of the louvres a firm tap. Nothing happened. I repeated the action twice more before the glass shattered inwards. I looked around, listening out for a door opening at one of the neighbour's houses, but heard nothing.

I moved on to the next louvre, and the next, breaking each of them quickly. Then I removed stray pieces of glass from the aluminium frame, making sure not to cut myself and leaned through the gap. Finding a table nearby, I used it for balance, crawling in, up to my waist, before pulling my legs through.

As I stood upright, I saw that I was in a sunroom. I was thankful that it would be easier getting out than in. All I'd have to do was open the back door.

I had climbed through so carefully that I hadn't even disturbed a framed picture on the coffee table. Now, I picked it up and examined the faces of a middle-aged couple and a teenage boy. I scanned the walls, which were covered with images of the same family.

Beyond the sunroom, I found the kitchen. It was clean and well organised, the morning's dishes still drying in the orange rack to the side of the sink.

I had already searched most of the house and was in the master bedroom, rifling through the chest of draws, when I heard a car pulling into the driveway. Pocketing a silver watch and a ring that held three glittering gemstones, I backed out of the bedroom, my heart thumping. 'It's okay,' I told myself. 'You've still got time.'

I ran down the short hallway and through the kitchen, reaching the back door just as I heard the keys turn in the front door lock.

I put my hand on the door handle and twisted. Nothing happened.

I realised now that the door had been deadbolted. I should have checked it the moment I'd broken in. Now I wouldn't be able to get it open, and it would take me too long to get back out the window.

Running back down the hall, I saw the front door begin to open and ducked into the room on my right. It was a bathroom. Closing the door quietly, I crossed the room. Now, I was facing a small window with a shelf below. It was covered with toiletries, which I swept away with a rough movement. Plastic containers clattered to the floor, while a perfume bottle shattered in the bathtub.

'If they didn't know there was somebody here before,' I thought, 'they do now.'

As I unlocked the window, the cloying smell of perfume filled the room. I thought about the bedrooms I'd searched. In one, a whole wall had been dedicated to karate trophies and memorabilia. Feeling a sudden rush of panic, I leapt up onto the windowsill. I was just about to climb down when I heard the bathroom door open behind me and a woman screamed.

Moments later, I was running towards the back garden, then through it, towards the tall fence at the back. I knew I would be able to climb it. I just hoped that it wouldn't be sharp on top.

I hadn't anticipated that I was being chased.

Just as I was about to leap for the fence, I heard footsteps behind me. Without turning around, I knew that it could only be the boy from the family photos. The same boy whose shelves were covered with martial arts trophies.

As I reached the fence, I felt his hands on my shoulders. Moments later, he was pulling me backwards, saying, 'No you don't!' Then he dragged me across the garden and tossed me into a lawn chair. He was breathing heavily, his fists clenched. I was afraid he was going to hit me, but somebody spoke and he looked at them above my head.

The voice belonged to a woman. She said, 'Have you got him? I've called the police.' Then she stepped into my line of sight and her eyes filled with pity. 'He's just a boy,' she said.

'He's a fucking thief,' her son said.

'Richie. Language.' The pictures in the sunroom hadn't done the woman justice. She had long, straight blonde hair and bright green eyes. After a moment, she picked up another lawn chair and placed it opposite mine. 'Are you okay?' she asked.

I nodded. The way she was looking at me now – that compassion – made me lower my eyes.

'What's your name?'

I knew what my dad would do. He would give her a false name, then look for the first chance to flee. Instead, I said, 'Peter.'

'What are you doing here, Peter?' she asked.

I reached into my pocket and produced everything I had stolen. On top was the engagement ring, which I handed back to her. 'My dad is in jail,' I said. 'I … I need money so we can find somewhere to live.'

The woman took the items I gave her, then handed them to her son, who continued to glare at me. She looked like she wanted to say something, but there were no words, really. We both knew that.

It took less than ten minutes for the police to arrive. I was surprised when the first officer to enter the backyard greeted the woman by name. He called her Leslie. In response, she stood up and spoke to him in hushed tones while another officer lifted me to my feet. I heard her say, 'Make sure you're gentle on him. He's had a bit of a rough trot, by the sound of things.'

'Do you want me to give Gary a call? Get him down here?' the officer asked.

'No,' Leslie said. 'It's all over now.'

The officer who was holding onto my arm laughed as he walked me down the side of the house. I glance at him and he shook his head. 'Robbing a Senior Detective's house,' he said. 'Well done!'

As we drove away from the house, lights on but siren off, the older officer told me there had been a string of 'B and E's' committed in the area in recent weeks. 'Was it you?' he asked.

I nodded.

'Righto,' he said, shaking his head disapprovingly.

When I entered the Shepparton Police Station, I remembered the last time I'd been here. Suddenly, I felt like I might throw up. This feeling only intensified when the officers led me into the same stark, white room where Kelly and I had been told we were being sent into juvenile detention. Kids' jail.

Now, I wondered whether I was headed back to Baltara. If so, I wouldn't be sent to Kinta. I'd be somewhere worse.

The officers left me alone for what felt like an hour before I heard the door handle turn and a short-haired woman entered the room. It was the same female officer who had delivered the news to me and my sister that night. Angela. Her auburn hair was longer now, and she had put on a few kilos. She still wore the same thick-rimmed glasses. 'Hello, Peter,' she said.

Without thinking, I jumped off my chair and threw my arms around her. Angela allowed me to hold her for a few seconds, even patting my back, before she extracted herself from my grasp and motioned for me to sit down again.

'This isn't exactly how I wanted to meet you again,' she said with a sad smile.

A wave of shame washed over me and I burst into tears, telling her, 'I'm so sorry.' I said other things – about feeling lost, about not knowing what else to do.

Angela rubbed my shoulder and let me speak. Finally, she said, 'Peter, you're facing more than a dozen charges for breaking and entering. Did you know that?'

I nodded.

'The officers told me that you've admitted what you did, which is a good thing, but this means that you're not going to be able to stay with your sister anymore.'

'Does she know what I did?' I asked, feeling like I'd been punched in the stomach.

Angela nodded. 'She's outside, with her husband. They've both been informed.'

As I started to cry once more, Angela's tone softened. 'You're very lucky, Peter,' she said. 'You could be sent to juvenile detention, but the woman whose house you broke into has some influence. She's reached out to a family that live a couple of hours away, at a dairy farm near Kyabram. They've agreed to look after you for a little while. They're good people.'

I took a deep, shaky breath, and thanked her.

Angela nodded. 'I have to tell you, Peter, if we see you here again, it's going to end very differently. Do you understand?'

I thought about the boys at Baltara, the ones who had already been there for years when I met them, who had grown up there. I didn't want to be like them.

'I understand,' I said. And I meant it.

# CHAPTER 16

# A PLACE TO CALL HOME

It was mid-afternoon when we passed through the small town of Girgarre and Angela said, 'Almost there.' On both sides of the road, pastures were filled with cows. Some were black, some brown, and some black and white. I watched them meander along, chewing the bright green grass, and thought that Kelly would love it here.

The car turned off the dirt road and began to climb up a driveway, the driver steering sharply to avoid the occasional pothole. At the top of the hill, we came to a fence, its wide gate standing open. A large, white sign read DULLARD.

Now, I could see a white weatherboard house. It was surrounded by a well-kept lawn.

As the car pulled to a stop, Angela said, 'Ready, Peter?'

Moments later, we climbed out of the vehicle. Angela opened the boot and handed me my bag. As I hoisted it onto my shoulder, the Dullard family came out to meet us.

In the car, Angela had told me what she knew about them. The parents were named Jack and Joan. They had six children, five of whom were already adults, ranging in age from their early-to-late twenties. Their names were Paul, John, Bernard, Kathryn and David. Only one, Elizabeth, was younger than me. She was ten.

Joan wiped her flour-covered hands on her floral-print apron and stepped forward, saying 'Peter!' in a tone that made it seem like we had met before. 'I was just baking Anzac biscuits. Would you like one?' As I nodded, Joan pointed to the oldest of her children, saying, 'Paul, take Peter's things into his room, please.'

With a hand placed gently on my shoulder, Joan steered me past the rest of her family and through the front door. I gave Angela a wave goodbye. Then I was walking ahead of Joan down a narrow hallway lined with family photos on one side and books on the other. As we walked, the smell of fresh-baked biscuits grew stronger, making my tummy rumble.

'That smells amazing, Mrs Dullard,' I said.

She laughed. It was a high-pitched laugh, like a train whistle, and was so surprising coming from her sturdy chest that I almost laughed in response. 'We don't stand on formality here, Peter,' she said. 'Call me Joan.'

'Okay, Joan,' I said, feeling myself relax immediately.

A couple of minutes later, I was sitting at the kitchen table, with a plate of biscuits and a cup of warm milk – cooked on the stove top rather than microwaved – in front of me. I chewed on a cookie and was washing in down with milk when Liz appeared at my elbow and asked whether I would like to play.

I glanced at Joan, who said, 'Go ahead, Peter. You can finish this later.'

I followed Liz back down the hallway to her room.

For the next two hours, we played a series of games with her meagre but well-kept toys. At one point, Joan brought my cookies and milk into the room and I devoured them between two games of checkers, both of which I won. Then it was time for dinner.

That night, as we ate, I met the rest of the family properly. They all worked on the farm, and explained the sorts of jobs they did, which I pretended to understand. Like his wife, Jack seemed friendly and welcoming. When he said that he'd been putting in a new fence all afternoon, I looked at the size of his hands and had a mental image of him sharpening a fence post and driving it into the ground using only his own strength.

That night, I slept more peacefully than I had in months.

Over the next couple of weeks, each day after everybody had finished work, we played cricket or kicked the footy in the backyard or rode motorbikes around the property. Sometimes Liz and I went off together, climbing haystacks in the barn or collecting eggs from the chook shed. My favourite activity was swimming at the local channel, where even the grown children still loved swinging over the water on a rope before performing daring backflips into the grey-green water below. I was amazed to see a family that had stayed together for so long, and was aware of how lucky I was to be invited to stay.

It didn't take me long to throw the Dullards' hospitality back in their faces, though. One Saturday night, I decided I was going to make the almost 20km trip into Kyabram alone, and without seeking permission from my foster parents. I waited until everyone went to sleep, then expertly laid pillows beneath my covers, and placed the head of a life-size golliwog doll on my pillow. Before leaving my room, I made sure that a couple of the doll's black curls could be seen above the duvet.

Outside, I walked into the carport and pushed Jacks' pride and joy, a pristine yellow Torana, down the driveway. I jumped in as it picked up speed, and guided it downhill, with the engine off, passing through the front gate and onto the road beyond with only the slightest thump of rubber. As the car's momentum began to slow, I switched on the engine and put it in gear, then pressed the accelerator gently. The car leapt forward with a purr.

A minute later, and I was far enough from the house to give the car more speed, my headlights illuminating the dusty road in front of me and an arc of farmland on either side.

Of course, there wasn't much to see in Kyabram so late at night. I drove up and down the deserted main street, then took a narrow road back out of town. All pretty harmless. A little after 2am, I drove back up the driveway, keeping the car's speed as low as I could without stalling the engine. Then, as soon as I reached level ground, I cut the engine and allowed the car to coast through the yard. I had already turned the headlights off, and navigated carefully towards where I knew the carport must be. After parking the car, I opened and closed the door as quietly as I could, then climbed back through my bedroom window and into bed.

The following morning, I was in a deep sleep when Joan woke me up. She was sitting on the end of the bed. 'Were you driving the Torana around Kyabram last night?' she asked, her tone matter-of-fact, but her eyes flashing with an anger I had never seen in them before.

'No,' I said, feigning confusion. 'Of course not.'

Her mouth formed a straight line. Then she took a deep breath and said, 'Well, Peter, the police are telling a different story. Apparently, somebody thinks they saw you driving. And, since you're underage, we've been asked to come down to the station.' She stood up. 'Get dressed, and we'll go and sort this out.'

On the way to the police station, I sat in the front seat of Joan's car, a Valiant sedan. Neither of us said anything. I knew that I had been found out and that I would just have to face whatever punishment was about to come my way.

When we walked into the Kyabram Police Station, I found myself staring down at the linoleum in front of my shoes. Then I told myself that this would only make me look more guilty and forced myself to look straight ahead.

After a brief wait, we were ushered into a back room, where an officer was waiting for us. He introduced himself as Sargeant Keoh. I expected the lecture to come entirely from him, but he glanced at Joan and she began instead. 'You didn't tell me the truth this morning, Peter,' she said. 'We both know that. And so does Sargeant Keoh.'

The way she was looking at me made me feel sick, suddenly. Her eyes were less accusing than they should be, and more hurt.

'I'm sorry,' I said.

Now, it was Sargeant Keoh's turn to speak. 'You know that you could have killed yourself, don't you, Peter?' he asked. 'You or somebody else?'

I nodded.

'And you know that this is a betrayal of trust? That you've betrayed the people who are trying to help you?'

Again, I nodded. I could feel the tears beginning to well up now and told myself not to cry.

'Well,' Sargeant Keoh said, 'You're lucky, Peter. Today, at least. Mrs Dullard has told me she doesn't want to press charges.'

I felt a wave of relief wash over me, but when I turned to offer Joan my thanks, she was no longer looking at me. My eyes began to sting.

'Thank you,' I told her. When she said nothing, I turned to Sargeant Keoh, who gave me a look that told me he understood how difficult it would be for me to mend things at home.

'You're welcome, Peter,' he said, graciously.

When we got home, John was washing the Torana, and glared at me as we drove past. I could see Jack working on the engine of one of the property's tractors, his eldest son by his side. As I closed my door and followed Joan towards the house, both turned their heads before Jack said something and Paul retrieved a wrench from the toolbox at his feet. I couldn't read Jack's expression, but I was sure he would be just as disappointed as Joan.

I fully expected my foster parents to call my caseworker in Perth that morning if they hadn't already done so.

The first chance we had to talk was lunchtime. Since arriving back at the farm, I had stayed in my room, avoiding everybody. I had tried to read a novel I'd found on one of the bookshelves, but my attention had kept wandering. I had asked myself, many times, why I had taken the car … what I had hoped to gain from it. But I had yet to come up with a good answer.

When Joan asked me to come into the kitchen for some lunch, I found Jack sitting at the table, a thick sandwich in front of him. Joan served me a pastie, then sat down beside her husband. They let me take a few bites of the pastie before Joan spoke.

'We'd like to have a bit of a chat, Peter,' she said.

I nodded. It wasn't like Joan to put off the inevitable. I knew that. Despite feeling like I knew what she was going to say, I resisted the urge to look away.

It was Jack who spoke next. 'We're not angry with you, mate,' he said. 'Do you think the other kids didn't do stupid things when they were your age?'

The relief I felt at these words made the pastry from the pastie catch in my throat, and I coughed suddenly, then took a sip of water to wash it down.

'We were thinking that it might be time to get you enrolled at St Augustine's,' Joan said. 'You're a smart boy, Peter. Anybody can see that. You don't want to be sitting around the house with nothing to do. Not if you're going to stay with us for the ... longer term, that is.'

For a few moments, I said nothing. Then I realised that Joan's final words were less a statement than a question. She was asking me what I wanted to do.

'I ... I would love that,' I said.

Joan took a deep breath and smiled. Then she placed her hand on top of Jack's, and said, 'We're glad, Peter. Lizzie will be, too. She'll love having a new friend she can show off at school.'

That night, I wrote to Dad and told him all about the Dullards. I admitted that I had taken the car, and explained that they had wanted me to stay anyway. I posted the letter the next morning at the nearest post box, and thought about Dad reading it while sitting in a mess hall or lying on his bed in jail. He felt a long way away now. Further than ever before.

A few days later, I found a letter addressed to me in my place at the table. I took it to my room and read my dad's response. He told me that he loved me and missed me, and encouraged me to listen to the Dullards and do what they told me. He said he was doing fine, but there was something in his tone that made me doubt this was true.

\*

My start to school, like most other things around that time, was a little shaky and uncertain, but I made friends relatively easy with Liz's help. After some negotiation between the Dullards and the Principal, Mr. Pattison, I had been enrolled in Year 8, despite being a younger than the rest of my classmates. I struggled with the schoolwork – particularly in Maths and Science – while I excelled in English, particularly when we got the opportunity to tell stories.

As a way to cover up my frequent confusion and frustration with my studies, I took on the role of class clown. On one occasion, I took the momentary absence of our History teacher to gather as many compasses from the students around me as I could. Then, after telling them to watch out, I turned then ceiling fan up to its highest setting, and began flinging the sharp metal objects upwards. Girls and boys hid, laughing, as the missiles rained from above, burying themselves – nib-first – in tables and chairs.

This preceded one of many trips to the Principal's office. Despite my clown-like demeanour in class, by the time I reached his office I was often angry, and Mr Pattison would make me sit and calm down before he spoke to me. He was always very understanding and kind, inevitably making me return to class with a promise that I would behave myself, which I fully intended to keep … for a short while, at least.

What I lacked in academics, I made-up for in my sporting prowess. I was fortunate to have natural talent and I could run all day. Having grown up in New South Wales, I had never played Aussie Rules, the Victorian game. That year, however, I joined the Kyabram team and loved it. More than the ability to run, pass and kick, I became a specialist at annoying the opposition, often causing them to make costly errors.

For the next few weeks, I spent my days studying at St Augustine's, my spare time at the local footy field, and mornings and evenings helping Jack around the farm. In my letters, I told Dad about life on the farm. In response, his letters became more desperate, filled with promises that our family would soon be back together. His handwriting took on the appearance of a hurried scrawl, and his sentences were filled with more and more spelling mistakes. I wanted to believe what he said – of course – but his promises had started to make me feel anxious. I got a tiny pit of dread each time I saw the small, pale yellow envelope waiting for me upon my return from school.

One morning, when we were gathering eggs together, Liz asked me what my life had been like before coming to live at the farm.

I had known that she must be curious, but she'd never asked me outright before. I wondered what to tell her. I thought about my time at Baltara, moving to Western Australia with my dad and my time at Kmart, living on the streets in Perth, and finally of the break-ins around Shepparton. 'It was pretty hard,' I said, finally. 'Sometimes I thought things would get better, but they never did. Not really.' When Liz looked at me with pity, I added, 'But it wasn't all bad. I had a full-time job for a little while. They made me a manager. They thought I was sixteen.'

She laughed as she placed an egg into the basket I held. 'No way!' she said. 'You'd never pass for sixteen!'

I laughed, too, as we left the chook shed and headed back to the house.

The following Sunday, I accompanied the rest of the family to church. I hadn't wanted to go before, and the family hadn't pressured me, but this morning I had asked Joan whether I could come along. 'Of course, Peter,' she'd said, looking quietly pleased. 'I've got some of the boys' old dress shirts in a cupboard upstairs. You can take your pick. You'll just need to iron it yourself.'

On the way to Church, Joan glanced at me in the rear-view mirror. I was squeezed between Liz and one of her brothers, feeling a bit uncomfortable where the starched collar of my shirt scratched my neck. 'Now, people are going to notice you today, Peter,' she said. 'You're an extra face. But you have every right to be there. If you like, you can call me mum.'

'Okay,' I said, automatically. I glanced at Liz, who gave me a small smile.

As well-intentioned as Joan's offer was, I knew that I would never feel right calling her mum. I already *had* a mum. Even if I hadn't seen her in more than a decade, she was still out there somewhere.

\*

A few days later, Joan drove me back to Shepparton, where I had been remanded to face charges at the children's court for the break and enters..

'Are you scared?' Joan asked as she parked her station wagon out the front of the Courthouse.

'A little,' I said.

As we exited the car, Joan took my hand and gave it a gentle squeeze.

Because I was still considered a State Ward, the Victorian Government had appointed a solicitor to take care of my case. He was a heavy-set man in his fifties, with a greying beard. He introduced himself to me as we headed into court but didn't wait for my response before addressing Joan. He spoke quickly and used a lot of legal jargon that I didn't understand. Looking at her expression, I was sure she didn't understand it either.

The solicitor addressed the Judge on my behalf and made all sorts of excuses as to why I behaved so badly. I had been placed in youth detention, I had been on the run with my dad and learnt bad habits. I had missed so much school and education and knew no better.

As he rolled off each excuse, I thought about the boy he was describing. He sounded like a hopeless case. But I knew that that wasn't true. Despite the claims of my solicitor, I knew that I had always had a choice – not over what had happened to me, of course, but over how I had responded to it. When I had done the wrong thing, it was because I *wanted* to.

It took less than ten minutes for the magistrate to hear my case and make his ruling. Despite my solicitor's claims, there was no doubt I was guilty. Before advising me of the outcome, he looked at me and said, 'In all my years on the bench, I haven't seen many 12-year-old kids who have performed as many criminal acts as you. Only time will tell if you are really a bad egg or just a kid who has had a horrible start to life.' He sentenced me to two years good behaviour and I was allowed to return to the Dullards' home.

Our solicitor shook my hand and Joan's and told us that it was a great outcome for us. Then he glanced at me for perhaps the first time all morning and said, 'Good luck,' before introducing himself to his next client.

When we returned to the farm and found Jack waiting for us, I was afraid he was going to ask me about the judgment. Instead, he opened Joan's door and kissed her on the cheek, then said, 'Peter, put some work clothes on and I'll meet you down at the sheds.'

By the sheds, Jack was referring to a milking complex at one end of the farm. It took me ten minutes to walk down there. When I arrived, I saw Paul and John already hard at work. Jack approached me and put a hand on my shoulder. 'Since you're not in school today, I figured you could help us out. Sound good?'

While I liked seeing the cattle in the fields, I had no desire to work with them up close. They were bigger and heavier than I had ever expected, and they had a habit of releasing their bowels to form a large, wet pat without warning. Jack directed me to put on a pair of gumboots, which were encrusted with dried manure.

Predictably, as I attempted to put the cups over their teats, I ended up splashed with wee and poo from the enormous animals. I resisted the urge to vomit, and forced myself to make sure the cups were placed properly, knowing that – if I didn't do so – they wouldn't work and Jack might be disappointed or even angry. It was as I was placing cups on my third cow that I heard Jack yell, 'Shit!'

I turned around and saw Jack standing behind a cow, his face, hands and shirt covered in manure. For a moment, I froze, feeling the almost impossible urge to laugh but not wanting to make fun of him. Then I saw John stand up and follow my gaze to where his father stood. Pointing, he shrieked with laughter and yelled, 'Paul! Check out the old man!'

Then Paul was laughing too, as was Jack, his teeth and eyes only just visible behind the dripping, brown mask.

Finally, my own laughter came in waves, tears rolling down my face. Every time I got myself under control, I would look up to see Jack still standing there, wiping his face to little effect. The only thing that helped was when he found a hose, then bent over and let the water sluice away the thick muck. 'Filthy bloody things!' he said, sending all of us into another fit of laughter.

Later that afternoon, exhausted but happy, I climbed on to the back of Jack's four-wheeler and we rode up the hill towards the house, following the cows. It was my task to close each gate behind them. As I waited for a straggler to pass through the final gate, I turned to look at the rolling pastures and the bright blue sky above.

I couldn't believe how far away this felt from my old life.

## Chapter 17

# THE FINAL CHOICE

After a couple of months living at the farm, I started dating Tamara. I had seen her around school, but I had never spoken to her until we were put in a group for a research project about Vikings. We arranged to visit the library after school and, while searching the stacks for relevant books, we discovered we both liked reading and sport and action films. I asked whether she'd like to go to the movies in Kyabram, and Joan drove us there the following Saturday. After that, we spent most lunchtimes together. I was happy the day she said she thought of me as her boyfriend.

Now, I had a new purpose. Several nights each week, I snuck out, wheeling the Ag motorbike down to the bottom of the driveway before kickstarting it and taking the backroads to her place. As the wind whipped my face, I thought about my brother Dave, and how free he had seemed those times he'd shown up on his motorbike. I fantastised that I looked that cool.

With Tamara by my side, school became something I started to look forward to. Bit-by-bit, my grades improved, and I built a great circle of friends, all of whom stood by me even though their parents had warned them away from 'that Norris boy'. Despite the Dullards' attempts to shield their own children and the town from knowledge about who I was, as in most small towns, word of my dad's exploits had travelled fast. I had no idea how much worse this was about to get.

I got my first indication of the trouble that was to come when Liz and I arrived home from school one afternoon to find a police car in the yard and Sargeant Keoh sitting at the kitchen table. 'Peter,' he said, 'Your dad has escaped from jail.'

Joan took over. 'What Sargeant Keoh needs to know, Peter, is if your dad has made contact with you. Other than the letters, I mean,' she said. For the first time, I noticed the small pile of envelopes on the table and felt a flash of anger. I would have given them to her, or to the officers, if they had asked. But it hurt to think that they had just taken them.

'No,' I said, honestly, then motioned to the letters. 'Everything I know is in those.'

My mind was racing. I remembered seeing Dad in the remand centre that day in Perth, the way he had promised that he would always come for me. I had no doubt he meant it.

Before he left, Sargeant Keoh made me promise that I would tell him if my dad tried to contact me in person. I told him I would. Of course, I had no intention of snitching. I had been trained better than that.

Two nights later, I was relaxing with the rest of the family in the living room. *Neighbours* had just finished, and we had just begun to watch *Australia's Most Wanted*. The show had been devised as a way for the Australian police to get the public's help in tracking down some of the country's most notorious crooks. When a picture of the featured criminal flashed onto the screen, my breath caught in my throat.

On screen was my dad's mugshot, accompanied by the name Clarence Donald Norris.

'Holy shit!' John said.

Joan entered the living room, saw what we were watching, and crossed the room, her hand extended as she prepared to turn the television off.

'No!' I said. 'Please. Leave it on.'

Turning to me, Joan pursed her lips, then sat on the end of the sofa, watching the show along with the rest of us.

The host informed viewers that Clarence Norris had escaped from Fremantle Prison and was presumed to be heading to Victoria. Viewers were advised that, if they saw him, they should not approach him; instead, they should call Crimestoppers.

As I looked at the familiar Crimestoppers number, I felt sad for Dad, knowing at that very time he was hiding somewhere, most likely without money or food. I knew that his only motivation would be to get back to me. And I knew, also, that the police were aware of this, and would no doubt be waiting for him if he ever showed up.

The next day, when Liz and I entered the schoolyard, there was a buzz of excitement. Many of the kids had seen the previous night's TV broadcast or, if they hadn't, had heard about it from those who had. Immediately, I was surrounded by kids, clamouring over each other.

'That's your dad?'

'How cool!'

'Do you know where he is?'

'He looked like a real badass!'

It was as I was trying to work out how to respond that Tamara approached and took me by the hand. She led me to a smaller courtyard where the rest of our friends were waiting. I didn't begrudge the other kids' curiosity. It was a small town, after all.

Beginning a few weeks before, Joan and Jack had given me permission to spend some time with my sister, Tina. Each time, they dropped me off on the Friday afternoon and collected me on Sunday morning. My next scheduled sleepover was the following weekend. As we drove away from the farm that Friday afternoon, I relished the opportunity to be somewhere I wouldn't have to answer questions about my dad.

When we reached Shepparton, I said goodbye to Joan, then knocked on Tina's front door. She welcomed me and told me I could put my bag in the spare room, which I did. I had returned to the kitchen and was about to ask for a cool drink when she said, 'I have a surprise for you, Pete. Get in the car.'

Ever since we were little kids, when my older sister told me to do something, I'd do it. This was no exception. I made my way to her car and buckled up in the front seat.

As we drove, she asked me the same questions as usual: was I was being looked after properly? Was I staying out of trouble? I told her I was fine, and assured her that the Dullards were good people. I meant it.

It was at this point that I realised how circuitous the route was that she was taking. In the last two minutes, we had circled the same block three time. 'What are you doing?' I asked.

Tina glanced in the rear-view mirror, then turned left, sharply, down a narrow street without using her indicator. As we reached the main road, she gave me a wink and said, 'You'll see, Petey.'

Finally, we pulled up outside a block of decrepit units. 'Come with me,' Tina said as she got out of the car. She walked through a narrow corridor between buildings, then marched up to door bearing the number 12a. I expected her to knock, but she produced a key from her purse and unlocked the door. Inside, the flat was unfurnished. I wondered what we were doing here.

'Just me!' Tina called out, shutting the door behind us.

Now, I became aware that we were not alone. I couldn't hear anybody else in the flat, but I could sense them somehow.

A moment later, a man stepped out of the hallway and into the living room and my eyes were flooded with tears.

'Dad!' I yelled, throwing my arms around him.

He wrapped me in the tightest hug I have ever felt.

'Petey!' Dad said, more a sigh than a word.

I stayed in his embrace for what felt like minutes before I finally let go. As I did, I looked at him carefully for the first time. He was skinnier than I remembered, his hair greyer, his face more gaunt. 'Are you sick, Dad?' I asked.

'No, no, Petey,' he said. 'You know nothing could take me down.'

While Dad and I sat on the floor and chatted, Tina went out. She came back half an hour later with some groceries, which she unpacked in the kitchen. Nothing was perishable, I noticed. Just cans of food, instant coffee and powdered milk. She'd bought three mugs, which she rinsed out before making us each a cup of coffee.

She had also brought board games. These weren't new, so she must have packed them in the boot of her car sometime before leaving the house. Without her husband knowing, I assumed. She'd chosen Monopoly, Risk and Pictionary, three of our favourites.

For the next two hours, Dad and I played Monopoly while Tina did her best to make the place feel a bit more comfortable, given the few basic supplies she'd managed to smuggle from her own home, including some cushions, a sleeping bag, and some bathroom essentials.

It was when we were playing, and Dad was losing – an unusual occurrence for somebody who had the combination of rabid competitiveness and the propensity to cheat – that he said, 'How's your other sister?'

I waited for him to finish the sentence – to say her name – but he didn't. Instead, he peered at the card he held as if he had never seen it before.

'Kelly?' I laughed, then said, 'What's the matter, Dad? Did you forget her name?'

As soon as I said the words, I regretted them. Dad looked at me, his eyes flashing, and said, 'Of course I bloody didn't. Don't treat me like an idiot!'

'I … I know, Dad,' I said. 'I'm sorry. It was just a joke.'

Realising he'd upset me, Dad put a hand on my arm. 'I'm sorry, son,' he said. 'It's been a … stressful time. That's all. I think it's … taking its toll.' Then he flashed me a grin. 'Now, give me my 200 bucks for passing GO!'

\*

This was the first of several such visits, during which Tina and I spent a few hours with Dad, eating and drinking, playing games, talking. During the week, I returned to the Dullards' place, but I no longer felt as if they were my family. I *knew* who my real family were. I found myself playing less with Liz, and doing my chores with a growing sense of resentment.

My new attitude didn't escape Tamara's notice. When she asked me what was wrong, I told her it was nothing. When she said that I didn't seem happy, I said maybe I wasn't. And, when she asked whether it was her, I just shrugged. I wanted to tell her that I didn't know what was wrong, but that would involve explaining everything, and I knew that I couldn't do that. We never officially broke up, but she didn't ask me to ride my motorbike over anymore and we stopped hanging around together at school. I threw myself into sports, going to the oval to play kick-to-kick every lunchtime, where I could be as rough as I liked in my pursuit of the ball.

The only one who might have suspected what was going on was Joan. Since our initial discussion with Sargeant Keoh, she had asked me a few times whether my dad had tried to contact me. I had assured her he hadn't. One afternoon, however, she asked whether she could see me in the kitchen. After presenting me with a plate of Anzac biscuits and a cup of warm milk, she said, 'You know you can tell me anything, don't you, Peter?'

I nodded, chewing a biscuit and keeping my gaze fixed on her while trying not to look her directly in the eyes.

'We are so proud of your efforts in school, and football. You're becoming quite the star player, I hear. Mrs Grunner, from the Chemist, said that you're being considered for Best and Fairest.'

This was the first I had heard of it. I felt a swell of pride, and immediately thought how good it would feel to tell my dad if, in fact, I received the honours.

Joan was speaking again. I did my best to focus on her words. For some reason, her eyes were filled with tears as she said, 'Regardless of whatever decisions you've made, and any you might make in the future, there will always be a home here for you, Peter. We love you.'

These words were still echoing in my ears when I met with Dad the following weekend. Joan had dropped me off as usual, and I had bounded into the house, ready to jump in Tina's car and head to Flat 12a. We waited for a few minutes to ensure that nobody was watching her unit, then left and took a new route.

Tina let us in.

'It's just us!' I called out.

Dad appeared, and I hugged him tightly. Tina said she had some errands to take care of, then left, closing the door behind her.

'Monopoly today, Dad?' I asked. Then I remembered something and reached into my backpack. Tina had asked me to pack a few more clothes than usual this time – 'in case you get cold' – and my bag was full. Even so, I had found room at the top to fit a packet of Tim Tams, Dad's favourite. 'Here,' I said, handing him the packet. 'I bought them with my pocket money.'

Dad took the biscuits from me with a tight smile. Then he said, 'Petey, take a seat.'

At some point over the last few weeks, Dad had rescued a half-broken couch from the nature strip. I sat down on it, trying to ignore the spring poking into my back. Dad's expression was serious as he said, 'This is all getting a bit risky, son. If I stay in Shep any longer, I'm bound to get caught.'

I asked whether Tina had any friends he could stay with, but Dad shook his head. 'The cops … they're not stupid.' He said, then smiled. 'Well, not entirely. If I stick around, they're bound to catch up with me sooner or later.'

Suddenly, I knew that Dad was leaving again. Immediately, I felt a sense of longing, for our hugs, out chats, our regular meetings, and was afraid I was going to start sobbing.

Seeing my expression, Dad said, 'Hey, hey.' He put his hands over mine. 'Don't cry. I don't want that.' Then he took a deep breath and said, 'There's a reason I told Tina to make sure you brought some extra clothes. It's time, Petey. If we're gonna get away from here, we need to go tonight.'

For a few moments, I said nothing. Then Dad pushed one of the curls from my forehead and said, 'You want to have some more adventures with your old man, don't you?'

I nodded.

He smiled. 'If we go tonight, we'll have the whole weekend before the Dullards report you missing and people realise what's happened.'

My stomach churned as I looked into my dad's eyes. For so much of my life, I had wanted nothing more than to look into his face each day and see him smiling back at me.

I had wanted him to choose me … which is what he was doing now.

But I was no longer that unhappy boy, living in foster homes, who yearned for escape. For the first time in my life, I felt almost settled. Almost happy.

*There will always be a home here for you, Peter. We love you.*

'Dad,' I began, then felt the tears come. I couldn't look at him as I said, 'I just … I just don't know …'

I heard my dad's breath catch in his throat.

'Petey,' he said, in a tone I didn't recognise. In it, I heard fear. Loneliness. 'You understand that I can't stay here, don't you? That I would do anything to stay if I could?'

I nodded. And yet, for the first time, I didn't believe him. Because, when he'd had the opportunity to be with me – with us – he had always chosen otherwise.

Of course, I couldn't say this to my dad. Even if I had been able to form the words, I would never have wanted to see the pain in his eyes. If I went with him now, I would be choosing to follow the same path. It would be exciting – an adventure – but it would mean hurting people, beginning with the Dullards. Either that, or I could choose my own path.

I knew now what I had to do.

I looked up, at the person who meant more to me than anybody else in the world, and said, 'No, Dad. No more adventures. I'm sorry.'

For a long time, he held my hands in silence. My fingers were small and narrow compared to his. Then, without another word, he stood up and crossed the room. I heard him take his keys out of his pocket, open the front door and close it quietly behind him. Moments later, he drove away. As I sat there, alone, I knew instinctively that I would never see my dad again.

For the second time in my life, a parent had left me. But this time, the choice was mine.

# EPILOGUE

My dad was many things: a crook, a liar, a cheat. But to me, he was just Dad. The guy who showed me how to ride a bike and mow the lawn. Who taught me to outrun the wind itself, barefoot no less. Yeah, he made a lot of bad choices, did things he shouldn't have, but he was also the one who tucked me in at night with Tom the Turtle, who high-fived my every little win.

Isn't it ironic that Fremantle Prison, the same place Dad escaped from by playing sick, ended up being his final resting place? He died in a prison medical unit at just 56-years-old from complications of Alzheimer's, only months after being extradited back to West Australia.

The day I found out still sits heavy in my heart. My sister Tina called to tell me, and just like that, I went numb. It didn't make sense. This was Dad we were talking about; the guy who'd ducked and weaved through every punch life threw his way.

I spent hours – days, even – walking around in a daze. I cried. I screamed. Then I reached a place where I could think again.

I'm not the church-going type, obviously, but there's a quote I once read about us all being tourists, and someone upstairs is already planning our whole trip, from start to finish. Makes me wonder if Dad's journey could've played out differently if he'd just turned right instead of left.

As a father myself, I've come to understand just how much Dad sacrificed to hold us together. That day in Unit 12a, when I finally chose to make a better life for myself, might've seemed selfish to him at the time, but I think he may have understood later.

Funnily enough, I wouldn't change a thing about my time with him, for which he deserves credit. We weren't living the high life – in and out of housing commission homes, emergency stays with the Salvos – but none of that mattered to me. Not really. When I was cuddled up to Dad, I was as happy as a kid could be. Those slow Sunday mornings, strolling hand-in-hand to the milk bar for that 20-cent bag of lollies, are my most cherished childhood memories.

It's always the simple stuff that sticks, isn't it?

For all his faults and fuck-ups, I've come to forgive my dad. How could I not? His choices weren't black and white, just different shades of struggle. Dad was a product of his rough upbringing and the hard knocks he faced. Yeah, he was once Australia's Most Wanted – no escaping that – but that's also the same man who showed me what it means to love and be loved, no matter what. I'll always be grateful for that. At the end of the day, he was just a bloke trying to protect his family the best way he knew how.

As for the rest of us … we're scattered across Australia, but we keep in touch.

Dave followed too closely in Dad's footsteps, unable to shake the gravitational pull of the underworld. He's done jail time but also worked as a gunsmith and a horse trainer. Today he lives in Kings Cross, where he's been for years. He has 3 beautiful daughters of his own, Sam, Amy and Georgia.

Tina, the teenage girl who defied death after falling from a motorbike without a helmet, is now a wife and mother. She lives in Noosaville, Queensland, with her husband Damien and their son Tyson. She still struggles with memories of our childhood.

I never thought I'd see Kelly again after we were torn apart on the tarmac at Shepparton Airport and forced into separate foster families. But blood proved thicker than any ocean of distance and time. She's still a gentle soul, the girl who loved animals and nature, never fussed about material stuff. She lives a nomad's life, selling crystals from her van.

And Mum …? Well, I've found a way to forgive her for leaving. Deep down, she was just a shattered soul searching for a better life. As a parent myself, I know she must have thought about us often, as I have of her. If I could, I'd tell her how much I love her. I would ask her to come and find me – us – and stop hiding.

Somewhere, somehow, I hope she found the peace and happiness that had eluded her.

From the start, the odds were stacked against me. Yet I was determined to break free from Dad's shadow. I knuckled down in school, looked past my childhood, and ended up graduating from La Trobe University with a degree in tourism and hospitality. Later, I earned tertiary qualifications in human resources and marketing – the first step towards becoming a most unlikely CEO. Today, I run a multimillion-dollar hospitality venue in regional New South Wales, employing more than a hundred locals and giving back to a community that's been hammered by floods and fires. As a manager, I use many of the same techniques that were instilled in me by my old Kmart boss, the one who told me as an 11-year-old boy that I'd be a leader someday.

That same sporty streak that had me chasing kids twice my size back then still runs through these fifty-one-year-old veins. I've won state and international medals in athletics, including pole vault. I even competed in the World's Toughest Mudder, getting pulled out with frostbite after running through a sub-zero night. I placed third in my age group at the Obstacle Racing World Titles in the U.S.A., and I've won numerous bodybuilding titles, most recently six golds at International Natural Bodybuilding Association Victoria. Celebrating these wins always ends the same way – a big, greasy Hawaiian pizza (extra pineapple, naturally) and a mountain of chocolate mousse. Old habits, right?

These days, I provide a safe, loving home for vulnerable kids as a respite carer, paying forward the monumental favour the Dullard family gave this lost boy all those years ago. Many kids in my care just crave simple things – a hug and a bedtime story. Some arrive physically and mentally broken due to domestic violence. It's amazing how a few days of kindness and unconditional love can impact someone. Simpler still is the peace of sleeping without fear of being hurt by someone who's meant to protect you.

What I do know of Dad's lasting legacy, if you will, is the supreme importance of love and loyalty. It has become an unbreakable creed I've carried into fatherhood with my two daughters, Chloe and Sophie, and as a father figure to the kids in my care. Becoming a parent has given me a greater perspective of the pain my mum and dad undoubtedly felt when they were separated from their children. I cannot imagine being apart from my girls; I love them both so much and look forward to seeing the beautiful women they will become.

Who knows where I'd be today if not for the Dullards? We've always kept in touch. Jack passed away after a short battle with cancer but Joan, pushing ninety, still lives on her own in Kyabram. Even if I never called her mum, she's been more of a mother to me than anyone. I hope she knows that. The whole Dullard family had a hand in shaping my future. From sneaky beers in the snooker room with Melissa Etheridge on repeat, to backyard footy games, I wouldn't be half the man I am without them. But, above all, Joan is the one I owe most. Even when I gave her every reason in the world to give up on me, she never did. She's helped dozens of kids through foster care over the years. I hope that, somewhere in that mix, I've made her proud.

Recently, I settled with the state of Victoria over the nightmare that was Baltara Reception Centre. Despite legislation shielding them from being sued for my placement in a juvenile detention centre – 'it was just how things were done back then' – my case was finalised in a settlement hearing with legal firm Slater & Gordon. The most disturbing part? The state's lawyers couldn't hear my opening statement. It was 'too difficult' for them. To this day, they haven't heard that statement, or issued an apology for the way I was treated, let alone all the other kids who walked into that hellhole before and after me.

Kelly still has skeletons from her time in female youth detention centres. I hope reading this story gives her the courage to seek closure. The brutal experiences that defined my childhood – the violence, the betrayal and the never-ending upheaval – could've easily sent me down the same dark, destructive road as my dad. So many times, the anger and hurt I heaved around as a kid on the cusp of adulthood nearly threw me off track for good. But I've learned that we don't have to be shackled by our backstory. As much as those experiences stung like hell, they also hammered some serious resilience into me from a young age, an unstoppable drive to overcome every roadblock life threw my way.

You could say life dealt our family one certifiably crazy hand. There's no sugar-coating the crimes, the violence, the brokenness. But we've shown glimmers of grit, love, and the power of the human spirit in our own weird ways. If you take just one message from the raw honesty of my story, let it be this: we all get the chance to rewrite our script, to find redemption. Our past doesn't have to dictate our future.

My journey from troubled teen to CEO and gold medal athlete might seem far-fetched, but I'm living proof you can change your destiny, against all odds. Those experiences that test us? For the most part, they're the ones that build our resilience, preparing us for the tough times we'll inevitably face. Most of all, I've learned that hatred and holding grudges just compound misery. It's acceptance and forgiveness, imperfect as they are, that finally set us free.

Some nights, when I'm alone, I gaze up at a sky filled with stars. In the stillness, I swear I can feel Dad next to me again. It takes me back to that night we sat atop the sun-baked metal of our stolen Valiant, somewhere in the desolate red heart of the Nullarbor, staring up at that same sky. We were tiny against the vastness, yet our bond as father and son burned brighter than any star above us.

# ACKNOWLEDGEMENTS

My story could not have been written without the amazing support people around me.

To Dobbo Bronagh, Luke and Emily, my gratitude towards each of you is something I will fail to express sufficiently. The belief you have all had in me, and my story, is something I will be forever grateful for.

To my daughters Sophie and Chloe, I hope reading my story gives you a greater understanding of the person I am. Having both of you by my side gives me the strength to take on any challenge. I love you both more than the words on this page will ever express.

To Ashisha, Dog and Tequila, my life is better for having the 3 of you in it. Life is a constant adventure and couldn't imagine a time where we are not all together.

Jazzy, I am the best version of myself with you in my life. Your support and belief in me is something I will never forget and be forever thankful for. You have never doubted any crazy idea I have come to you with, you have stood by me through all of this. I love you.

## Peter Norris

# ABOUT THE AUTHOR

Peter Norris is not your ordinary CEO. The head of Club Corowa, a multimillion-dollar venue that employs more than 100 staff, he is also a world-class athlete who's won bronze in the Obstacle Racing World Championships and multiple national bodybuilding titles and he's the son of one of Australia's most notorious bank robbers.

Refusing to follow in his father's footsteps, Peter broke free from his shadowy past and forged a bright future. He graduated from La Trobe University with a business degree that launched his leadership career in the hospitality industry. He overcame the obstacles that threatened to derail and eventually destroy him, transforming barriers into breakthroughs.

As a former State Ward, he now provides a safe and secure home for vulnerable children and young people as a dedicated foster carer. He is also a motivational speaker, sharing his inspiring messages of resilience and redemption with audiences across Australia.

In a journey that spans far beyond the boardroom, Peter is living proof of how one man can change his destiny and make a difference; not despite the odds, but because of them.

To learn more about Peter www.thebankrobbersboy.com.au He'd love to connect with you!

For more great titles visit

**www.bigskypublishing.com.au**